The Journey of Coaching Miracles

(Transforming Lives Beyond Limits)

Author Introduction

Shipra is an International coach who is well-known for her steadfast commitment to empowerment and personal development. Shipra has over decade of expertise in coaching, mentoring, and personal development. She is known for being a transformative coach who helps people from all areas of life make significant and long-lasting changes.

Shipra's deep passion for enabling people to reach their greatest potential and lead fulfilling lives served as the driving force for her decision to become a coach. Her path is supported by a strong educational foundation that includes computer engineering, law, and counselling psychology. This background gives her a well-rounded viewpoint that she applies to her coaching.

Shipra's renowned title of "Mrs Universe Creativity" from the "Mrs Universe 2023" pageant is proof of her extraordinary accomplishments and shows off her grace and inventiveness on a global platform. To top it off, her titles as "Mrs India Glamourous Face" and "Mrs India Glamorous Goddess," along with her ranking as the second runner-up in "Mrs India," highlight her extraordinary abilities and services to the pageantry community.

Beyond her successes in the pageant industry, Shipra has a significant global influence. In her roles as POSH (Prevention of Sexual Harassment) Trainer, Image Consultant, and Soft Skill Trainer, Shipra is dedicated to supporting individuals' complete personal development and establishing nurturing environments that promote empowerment.

In "The Journey of Coaching Miracles," Shipra condenses her vast knowledge and experience into an engrossing tale replete with life-changing lessons, inspirational tales, and pragmatic counsel. Shipra guides readers toward clarity, confidence, and purposeful action by inviting them to go on a deep journey of self-discovery through her kind and approachable style.

Come along on this life-changing journey with Shipra as she gives you the tools to realize your full potential, get past challenges, and live a life full with opportunities.

Table of Contents

Book Introduction

Amidst all the noise of responsibilities and demands, there is a word that can be heard in the busy streets of today. It talks about unrealized potential, hidden hopes, and parts of the soul that haven't been explored yet. This quiet voice is inviting us to go on a journey of self-discovery, a trip that will awaken the miracles that are already inside us.

Let us take this chance to welcome you to "The Journey of Coaching Miracles," a trip that explores the power of coaching to change lives. Shipra Singh is the leader of this journey. She is a respected coach and wise author whose own life has been changed by the powerful effects of coaching on her and many other people's lives.

Shipra Singh wants you to read this book and start a path of self-realization and empowerment. You will go beyond what you think is possible on this journey, which will lead you to a life full of meaning, passion, and endless possibilities.

We will take a look at the different areas of human experience, one part at a time, and look into the depths of our lives and the heights of our hopes. Each part is like a compass that points us in the direction of our true north, which is becoming our best selves. This includes things like seeing our full potential, being true to ourselves, dealing with obstacles, and enjoying the things we've accomplished.

People who read this book will find useful information, moving stories, and life-changing tasks that are meant to awaken the greatness that is already inside you. As a coach, Shipra draws from his own life experiences as well as the knowledge he has learned from working with people from all walks of life over the years.

But this book isn't just about changing yourself; it's also about giving the group as a whole more power. Realizing how all living things are linked and the positive effects that happen when one person steps into their power and shines their light is what this is all about.

I hope that as you read these pages, you will find the drive to appreciate the beauty of your life, to follow your dreams, to overcome your obstacles, and to make a future that is beyond anything you could have imagined.

So, are you ready to go on this journey of coaching wonders, my reader? Do you think you're ready to let out the tremendous potential that's inside you? If that's the case, let's set sail together toward a horizon that's full of future prospects and hope.

Hey, welcome to the ship!

It's Shipra Singh.

Epigraph

Let us always meet each other with a smile, for the smile is the beginning of love. Through love and compassion, we can transform lives, illuminate paths, and create miracles in the hearts of others."

Mother Teresa

Life is a celebration of possibilities, a journey of self-discovery, and a canvas waiting to be painted with the colour of our dreams. With courage, grace, and determination, we can turn our aspirations into realities, and our dreams into miracles."

Sushmita Sen

Nothing is impossible in life, be unstoppable.

Surendra Narayan Singh
(My Father-Shipra Singh)

Forward

There are few journeys as personally enriching and impactful as the one undertaken by a coach. It's with immense enthusiasm that I congratulate Shipra Singh on the publication of her remarkable book, "The Journey of Coaching Miracles: Transforming Lives Beyond Limits."

Through my experience as an international Personal Impact Coach, image consultant, and etiquette trainer, I've witnessed first-hand the transformative power of coaching. Shipra Singh beautifully captures this essence in her book, offering readers valuable insights, practical exercises, and heartfelt reflections to guide them on their path to self-discovery and empowerment.

Shipra's own journey and expertise inspire readers to embrace authenticity, build confidence, and pursue their passions with unwavering purpose. Her commitment to empowering others shines through every page, encouraging readers to conquer challenges and live their dreams.

As a Personal Impact Coach, I deeply understand the importance of self-image and self-expression in achieving success and fulfilment. "The Journey of Coaching Miracles" echoes this sentiment, highlighting the role coaching plays in enabling readers to navigate life's obstacles with grace, confidence, and a genuine sense of self.

I have no doubt that "The Journey of Coaching Miracles" will serve as a source of inspiration and motivation for readers, propelling them towards a future brimming with possibilities. Here's to embarking on a journey of self-discovery, growth, and limitless potential.

Warmly,

Chinha

Chinha Raheja
Personal Impact Coach

Dedication

This book is devoted to the esteemed individuals who have played a pivotal role in my personal and professional development. I would want to thank all of my coaches, mentors, and teachers for their unwavering support, invaluable advice, and profound influence on my journey.

Nothing is impossible in life; be unstoppable! My father has been the one who has always inspired and motivated me. I would want to express my sincere gratitude to my father, family, friends, and husband, whose unwavering support and unwavering presence have been a source of inspiration and motivation for me throughout this journey. Your belief in me has given me more motivation to pursue my goals with steadfast devotion and to always aim for excellence.

With sincere gratitude and the greatest acknowledgement,

Shipra Singh

Purpose of the Book

*"The Journey of Coaching
Miracles"*

*(Transforming Lives Through
the Power of Coaching)*

In order to provide individuals who are interested in embarking on a transforming journey toward self-realization and empowerment with a guiding light, "The Journey of Coaching Miracles" was written with the intention of serving with this goal. This book digs deeply into the enormous impact that coaching may have on unlocking the underlying greatness that is present in every human. It is founded on the premise that every person holds potential that has not yet been fully realized and is waiting to be released.

The book "The Journey of Coaching Miracles" sheds light on the numerous ways in which coaching can stimulate both personal and professional development by weaving together a variety of real-life experiences, illuminating case studies, and practical activities. It investigates the role that coaching plays as a catalyst for transformation, enabling individuals to break free from limits that they have imposed on themselves, triumph over challenges, and embrace their actual selves with bravery and honesty.

At its core, the purpose of this book is to encourage readers to create a growth mindset, accept vulnerability as a source of strength, and navigate the challenges that life presents with perseverance and drive. The reader is provided with the tools, insights, and tactics necessary to travel their own unique route towards fulfilment and success. This is accomplished by delving into major themes such as recognizing potential, breaking barriers, and celebrating accomplishment.

In addition, "The Journey of Coaching Miracles" places a strong emphasis on the significance of connection and community in the coaching process. For the purpose of supporting personal development and communal empowerment, it underlines the power of supportive networks, meaningful relationships, and experiences that are shared by individuals. Readers are encouraged to investigate the tremendous influence that connection and cooperation can have on their journey toward self-actualization by examining the topic through the perspective of coaching.

In the end, the objective of "The Journey of Coaching Miracles" is to arouse a spark within each and every reader, so directing them toward a more profound comprehension of themselves, their goals, and the boundless potential that lies within them. For the objective of empowering individuals to embrace their authenticity, pursue their passions, and create a life that is filled with purpose, meaning, and joy, it seeks to empower individuals. This book provides you with vital ideas and inspiration to help you go on your own journey of coaching miracles, regardless of whether you are a coach, a client, or simply someone who is on a search for personal improvement.

1.The Power OF Coaching Miracles

Coaching is not only about achieving our objectives; rather, it is about having faith in ourselves, confronting our anxieties, and figuring out what our genuine potential is.

Welcome to the book **"The Journey of Coaching Miracles: Transforming Lives Beyond Limits!"** I am thrilled to have this opportunity to welcome you and share in the excitement of this incredible journey. This book aims to explore a variety of extraordinary stories that showcase the transformative power of coaching in people's lives.

One example to consider is Milkha Singh, a well-known Indian athlete who is also referred to as the "Flying Sikh." It was not from the beginning that he was a champion. In spite of this, he was able to make his ambitions come true and compete in the Olympic sprinting competition with the assistance of a coach. His story demonstrates to us that coaching may assist us in accomplishing remarkable things, regardless of where we initiate the process.

Coaching has always been an important factor in assisting individuals in accomplishing their objectives, from traditional tales such as the Mahabharata to contemporary achievements. Having this is similar to having a beacon that illuminates the path ahead of us when things become difficult.

In light of this, let us not forget that coaching is not only about achieving our objectives; rather, it is about having faith in ourselves, confronting our anxieties, and figuring out what our genuine potential is. Join me on this voyage of coaching miracles, and together we will discover how it has the potential to impact our lives in ways that we never imagined were possible.

1.1 Understanding the Power of Coaching

Coaching and the Role of a coach: The collaborative practice of coaching involves a coach and a client with the ultimate goal of reaching goals and realizing potential. In contrast to counselling or therapy, coaching doesn't delve into past traumas or concerns; instead, it concentrates on the present and future. It is results-driven, results-oriented, and progressive.

For their customers, a coach acts as a partner in accountability, guidance, and mentoring. They offer assistance, motivation, and helpful criticism to help people overcome challenges, define their objectives, and create successful plans. By means of attentive listening and insightful questioning, coaches enable their clients to find answers on their own and take significant action.

1.2 Transforming Lives Through Coaching

Individuals are given the ability to fulfil their full potential and achieve success in numerous aspects of life through the process of coaching, which has a tremendous impact on the transformation of lives across a variety of industries. Coaching can lead to transformation in a variety of various aspects of life, including the following:

Discovering Potential: Coaching has the effect of assisting individuals in recognizing and utilizing their inner potential, so directing them toward self-discovery and personal development. Sachin Tendulkar, who is widely considered to be one of the best cricketers of all time, was able to uncover his talent and refine his skills with the help of trainers beginning when he was a child. This led to a famous career in the sport of cricket.

The Overcoming of Limiting Beliefs and the Breaking of Barriers: Coaching has a significant impact because it gives individuals the ability to confront and triumph over limiting ideas that prevent them from reaching their full potential. As an illustration, Arunima Sinha, who was the first female amputee to climb Mount Everest, triumphed over the expectations of society as well as her physical limits with the assistance and direction of her coach, ultimately accomplishing her goal despite the fact that it was extremely difficult.

Recognizing the Value of Authenticity and Discovering the Power in Vulnerability: Coaching has a significant impact because it teaches individuals to accept and appreciate their true selves, which in turn helps to cultivate strength and resilience via acceptance of vulnerability. The journey of self-discovery and authenticity that Mahatma Gandhi undertook, which was guided by his inner voice and teachers, resulted in the enormous impact that he had on the movement within India to achieve independence.

Constructing Resilience in the Face of Adversity: Strategies for Overcoming Obstacles
Coaching has a significant impact on individuals because it enables them to develop the resilience and coping techniques necessary to navigate the challenges that life presents with grace and resolve. PV Sindhu, the Olympic badminton champion for India, overcame a number of obstacles and disappointments on her way to success. However, she persisted with the help and guidance of her coach, and as a result, she was able to achieve greatness on the international scene.

Coaching helps individuals clarify their goals and objectives, providing direction and support to turn their aspirations into actual achievements. This is the impact of coaching.

Empowering objectives: Coaching is a powerful tool. By persevering, working hard, and receiving direction from mentors who believed in his ability, Dr. APJ Abdul Kalam, also known as India's Missile Man and a former President, was able to transform his childhood ambition of being a scientist into a reality.

Developing Your Self-Assurance and Taking Control of Your Situation. Coaching has a significant impact on individuals because it increases their self-confidence and self-belief, which in turn enables them to venture beyond of their comfort zones and pursue their goals with bravery. Kalpana Chawla, the first woman of Indian descent to travel to space, was able to break down boundaries and shoot for the stars because she drew strength and confidence from her upbringing and the inspiration she received from her mentors.

Establishing Connections and Establishing Networks of Cooperation: The impact of coaching is that it makes it easier for individuals to build strong personal and professional networks, which in turn provides them with essential support and resources that will help them achieve their goals. As an illustration, Ratan Tata, who is widely regarded as one of the most influential business executives in India, developed a broad network of mentors and advisors who served as a source of guidance and support throughout his distinguished career. This network was important in the success of the Tata Group.

The Celebration of Success: Acknowledging Significant Milestones and Accomplishments
Coaching has a significant impact because it helps individuals to celebrate their development and achievements, which in turn fosters a sense of fulfilment and motivates individuals to continue their growth. Mary Kom, the boxing star of India and the Olympic bronze medallist, celebrates each milestone in her path with thanks and humility, thereby motivating others to continue in the face of adversity.

Sustaining Growth and Transformation While Exploring New Possibilities While Going Beyond Limits: Coaching opens up new possibilities for growth and transformation, empowering individuals to continuously evolve and reach new heights of success. Example: Swami Vivekananda, a spiritual leader and philosopher, embraced a life of continuous learning and self-improvement, guided by his spiritual mentors, leading to his profound impact on Indian society and beyond.

In the following chapters, we will go into each of these significant themes in greater depth, investigating the stories of individuals who have directly experienced the transformative power of coaching in their own lives. In this course, we will explore the complex process of personal growth and development that is aided by coaching. This will be accomplished through a combination of real-life examples, case studies, practical activities, and reflections.

You will be able to apply the insights, methods, and concrete steps that are provided in each chapter to your own lives. Each chapter will provide a comprehensive exploration of the relevant issue. We are going to embark on a journey across the varied landscape of coaching miracles, which will include everything from discovering hidden potentials to breaking through boundaries, embracing authenticity, managing challenges, and celebrating achievement.

We will investigate the ways in which coaching enables individuals to realize their full potential, triumph over challenges, and begin on a journey of unending development and transformation.

2. Discovering Potential: Unleashing the Power Within

> Coaching is all about being a guiding light, illuminating the path to self-discovery and empowerment.

As we dive further into the exciting journey of self-discovery and empowerment, we are building upon the strong foundation established in Chapter 1. Coaching is all about tapping into the untapped potential that lies within each and every one of us. It's about unleashing that hidden power and watching it soar to new heights. This belief forms the very foundation of the coaching profession.

In the opening chapter, we delved into the exciting concept of coaching miracles and their incredible power to ignite transformative shifts in people's lives. Hey there! Let's dive right into the exciting topic of discovering potential, a crucial part of the coaching process. Get ready to explore and unleash your hidden talents!

Just like coaching, the process of uncovering your potential is an incredible journey of self-discovery and empowerment. It's a transformative experience that guides you towards your true potential.

Join us as we embark on an exhilarating journey through the pages of Chapter 2! We invite you to embark on your own thrilling voyage of self-discovery. Get ready to dive into a world of self-discovery! We're here to help you explore your skills, passions, and objectives through practical tasks and reflective prompts. It's time to unleash your potential! Discovering the hidden gems within themselves is an exhilarating journey you embark on.

Just like Arjuna sought guidance from Lord Krishna on the battlefield of Kurukshetra, you are encouraged to embark on their own exciting journey of self-discovery, with the empowering support that coaching can offer. As individuals embrace their true selves and unleash their inner potential, they are paving the way for a future filled with endless possibilities, purpose, and ultimate fulfilment.

Hidden within the vast tapestry of human existence lies a boundless wellspring of untapped potential, eagerly yearning to be discovered. Each individual has a unique combination of abilities, talents, and passions just waiting to burst forth into the world! But often, this incredible potential remains untapped, hidden beneath layers of self-doubt, fear, and societal expectations.

Coaching is all about being a guiding light, illuminating the path to self-discovery and empowerment. Embark on an exhilarating journey of self-discovery and unleash your hidden potential through the transformative power of coaching! Get ready to dive into the exciting world of uncovering your true potential! We'll take a thrilling journey through the vibrant tapestry of Indian culture and history, drawing inspiration every step of the way.

2.1 Illustration with Example

Let me provide you with an illustration to better explain the concept.

Come on, let's dive into the ancient epic of Mahabharata and discover the incredible teachings of the Bhagavad Gita and how they relate to the coaching process!

Get ready to dive into the captivating tale of **Arjuna**, the fearless warrior prince, who found himself grappling with a profound sense of purpose on the battlefield of Kurukshetra. Filled with uncertainty and a deep sense of moral conflict, Arjuna sought the counsel of his charioteer, Lord Krishna. Arjuna's current state of vulnerability showcases the raw human experience of battling with self-doubt and uncertainty. It's a theme that strikes a chord with anyone on their personal quest for self-discovery.

With the wisdom of the Bhagavad Gita, Krishna takes on the role of a mentor, providing Arjuna with invaluable advice and support to conquer his inner conflicts and unlock his full potential as a warrior and a leader.

Krishna shares profound wisdom with Arjuna, highlighting the significance of embracing one's dharma, or righteous duty, and taking bold and resolute action in accordance with one's authentic self. Through harnessing his inner power and embracing his true calling as a warrior, Arjuna experiences a surge of clarity, determination, and a deep sense of purpose. With newfound purpose, he emerges from his existential crisis, prepared to embrace his destiny on the battlefield.

Arjuna's journey is an incredible metaphor for the coaching process, where individuals bravely face their inner demons, conquer their fears, and discover their untapped potential. By reflecting on themselves, seeking guidance, and exploring their own potential, people like Arjuna can unlock their inner power, embrace their special abilities, and achieve their greatest dreams.

> Call for Action: Reflect on own moments of doubt and uncertainty, and to explore how the teachings of the Bhagavad Gita can serve as a source of inspiration and guidance on your own path of self-discovery.
>
> Tap into your inner wisdom, embrace your true potential, and unleash the power within.

2.2 Illustration with Example

Let's dive into the incredible story of **Rani Lakshmi bai of Jhansi**, a fearless queen who became a powerful symbol of resistance during the Indian Rebellion of 1857. Follow the path that Rani Lakshmi bai took and witness the incredible power of coaching. It will unlock your true potential and empower you to lead with bravery and perseverance, even in the face of adversity!

Rani Lakshmi bai never let herself be consumed by despair, even when faced with numerous challenges and the oppressive rule of the British East India Company. With boundless energy and unwavering determination, she tapped into her inner reservoirs of resilience and courage. Harnessing her innate strength, she fearlessly led her people in their fight against the oppressive grip of colonial rule.

When we take a closer look at Rani Lakshmi Bai's journey through the lens of coaching, we witness the incredible growth of her leadership skills and the remarkable realization of her boundless potential as a visionary leader. Rani Lakshmi bai fully embraced her innate qualities of bravery, determination, and resilience, harnessing them to ignite a spirit of rebellion among her people, urging them to stand up against oppression. Just like a coach empowering individual to identify and make the most of their strengths, Rani Lakshmi bai did exactly that.

Rani Lakshmi Bai's unwavering determination and unwavering dedication to her people serve as a testament to the power of coaching in fostering transformative leadership, even in the face of seemingly unbeatable challenges. With the right guidance, she discovered the path she needed to follow and gained the confidence to lead with determination and passion. This coaching experience ignited a rebellious spirit within her that would go on to shape the future.

> Call for Action: Contemplate the life of Rani Lakshmi bai and think about the ways in which coaching ideas might be applied to your own lives.
>
> Tap into your inner strength, embrace your true potential, and unleash the power that is within you in order to bring about positive change in your own life and communities.

2.3 Discovery Exercise

You will be able to uncover your most profound passions and interests with the assistance of this activity, which will ultimately lead you to a life that is more purposeful and meaningful.

In the beginning of the exercise dealing with the discovery of passions, you are encouraged to set aside specific time for the purpose of introspection and reflection. The goal is to discover periods in your life when you felt the most alive and engaged.

Step 1: In order to set the stage:

a)   locate a place that is calm and comfortable, where you may engage in contemplation when there are no interruptions.

b)   Think back on times in your life when you experienced a profound sense of joy, fulfilment, or excitement. Recall moments of delight. It's possible that these times are connected to hobbies, activities, relationships, or events that brought you a great deal of delight and fulfilment.

c)   Identify Patterns: Recognize any recurring ideas or patterns that come to light as a result of your thoughtful considerations. Is there a particular activity or interest that you engage in on a regular basis that brings you happiness and satisfaction? In what ways do these encounters reflect the underlying ideals or passions that exist?

d)   Explore Curiosities: Investigate any hobbies or curiosities that you may have been fascinated about but have not yet pursued. Think about how you may incorporate these hobbies into your daily life and to discover new paths for growth and exploration.

e)   Imagine Your Ideal Day: Picture yourself in your ideal day, which would be full of experiences and activities that are in line with your respective passions and interests. In what way would you be acting? Together with whom would you be? Is that how you would feel?

By participating in this activity, you will be able to visualize a life that is in harmony with your most profound wants and goal.

Step 2: Develop a Plan of Action: Develop a plan of action through which you can incorporate your interests into your everyday life. Among these are the establishment of particular objectives, the identification of challenges and impediments, and the formulation of ideas for overcoming these situations. For the purpose of pursuing your passions and creating a life that is truly meaningful and rewarding, you should take tiny, concrete steps toward achieving your goals.

This journey will allow you to unlock the potential that lies within you to create a life that is purposeful, fulfilling, and joyful.

2.4 Self-Reflection

Take some time to pause and think on the path that you have travelled on your own journey of self-discovery.

- Which of your qualities and talents do you stand out the most?

- What latent passions do you have buried deep within you, just waiting to be uncovered? Take a moment to picture yourself in the future that you want.
- In your opinion, what does it mean to be successful?
- What are some ways that you might tap into your inner strength to bring about the life that you want?

While you are embarking on this life-altering path of self-discovery, it is important to keep in mind that the ability to realize your full potential is within you. You have the opportunity to tap into your innate strength, embrace your true identity, and go on a path that leads to growth, fulfilment, and empowerment if you engage in self-reflection, get direction, and receive coaching.

3.Breaking Barriers: Overcoming Limiting Beliefs

Limiting Beliefs are the attitudes and ideas that deplete your confidence and prevent you from pursuing your true desires.

Welcome to the exciting third chapter of our journey towards transformation! Today, we will dive deep into the invisible obstacles that can hinder our personal development and fulfilment. Get ready for an enlightening exploration! In this chapter, titled "Breaking Barriers: Overcoming Limiting Beliefs," we dive into the incredible impact that self-imposed constraints can have on unlocking our true potential. Get ready to explore the power of breaking free from these limitations!

Let's keep the momentum going as we dive deeper into our investigation, drawing inspiration from timeless coaching principles and a diverse range of real-life examples, just like we've been doing in the previous chapters. Now, let's dive into the exciting topic of internal roadblocks that often hinder individuals from reaching their goals. We'll build upon the foundation laid in Chapters 1 and 2 to explore this fascinating subject.

In Chapter 1, "The Power of Coaching Miracles," we introduced the concept of coaching as a catalyst for transformation. We wanted to share the idea of coaching with you. Let's dive into how coaching can help you uncover your strengths and talents, and unleash the incredible potential that lies within you! In Chapter 3, we dive into the common obstacles that often hold people back from fully embracing their true potential. In this chapter, we tackle those limiting beliefs head-on!

As we dive into Chapter 2, "Discovering Potential: Unleashing the Power Within," I want to energize you to explore your own hobbies and interests. The aim is to help you uncover the unique talents and abilities that reside within you. However, embracing and accepting oneself can be quite a journey filled with obstacles. When people are chasing their dreams and goals, they might come across some pesky beliefs that hold them back. Chapter 3 is where we dive into these exciting beliefs!

You can be seriously hindered by limiting beliefs. These are the attitudes and ideas that deplete your confidence and prevent you from pursuing your true desires. These ideas have presented serious difficulties for people at various points in history and across cultural boundaries. We may be seriously hindered by these difficulties and unable to achieve the contentment and happiness we so much want. Fear of failing, self-doubt, and the weight of societal expectations are just a few of the things that can impede our progress and prevent us from experiencing true joy.

Get ready to dive deep into the human mind as we explore the transformative power of self-awareness and empowerment. We're here to inspire you to challenge your own limiting beliefs and discover new possibilities. You are encouraged to tackle your own limiting beliefs head-on! To embark on a journey of personal growth, strength, and renewed motivation, we need to recognize and face the challenges that come our way.

Get ready for an exhilarating journey in this chapter! You'll be guided through a process of deep introspection and self-reflection, where you'll uncover and challenge those bothersome limiting beliefs that have been holding you back. You'll be empowered to overcome those bothersome negative thought patterns and self-doubt that are holding you back from achieving your goals. Get ready to dive into real-life examples and hands-on activities that will help you conquer those obstacles!

3.1 Illustration with Example

Let's dive into the remarkable life of **Sudha Murthy**, a renowned philanthropist and novelist, to showcase the incredible power of determination and resilience in defying societal norms and gender stereotypes.

Sudha Murthy's incredible journey is a testament to the unwavering human spirit and our ability to overcome self-imposed limitations that can hinder our personal growth. Sudha Murthy never let these limiting beliefs hold her back, even though she faced immense societal pressure and gender biases that tried to prevent women from pursuing education and professional opportunities. She forged her own path in life with unwavering determination and a strong belief in her own abilities.

As a young woman in India, Sudha Murthy faced numerous challenges that she had to overcome in order to achieve success. Sudha Murthy defied societal norms and pursued her passion for engineering, despite the restrictions placed on women in her society. Regardless of the scepticism and criticism she faced, she remained unwavering in her commitment to her goals and aspirations.

Sudha Murthy's journey was filled with triumphs over obstacles, leading her to remarkable success as an engineer, author, and advocate for social change. She accomplished this by staying unwavering and resolute throughout her journey. She shattered stereotypes and paved the path for future generations of women to chase their dreams, defying societal expectations and cultural norms.

This story is a powerful reminder of how tenacity and dedication can transform lives and help us overcome our own limiting beliefs. With her unwavering determination to defy societal norms and her relentless pursuit of change, she showcased the power of self-belief and triumphing over adversity.

Call for Action: examine the limiting beliefs that you hold and to think about the ways in which you might overcome challenges on your own path to achievement.

You have the ability to liberate yourself from the shackles of limiting beliefs and realize your full potential by engaging in self-reflection, demonstrating determination, and maintaining a firm faith in your own capabilities.

3.2 Real Life case Study

We dive into the inspiring journey of **Rahul, a young professional with big dreams and aspirations.** However, he finds himself grappling with self-doubt and a fear of failure. Join us as we explore how Rahul overcomes these limiting beliefs and breaks through barriers to achieve his entrepreneurial goals. Rahul's story is a powerful example of how coaching can help individuals break free from their limiting beliefs and develop a growth mindset. Through coaching, he was able to achieve his aspirations and overcome obstacles along the way.

Rahul's journey starts with a burning desire to launch his own company, driven by the ambition to create something meaningful and impactful. Meanwhile, Rahul is grappling with a wave of self-doubt and anxiety as he contemplates the idea of diving into the realm of entrepreneurship. There are some doubts about his abilities, he seems to be quite concerned about the potential dangers involved, and he appears to be a bit hesitant to pursue his aspirations.

In this pivotal moment, Rahul decides to consult a coach to enhance his performance. Coaching empowers Rahul to tackle his limiting beliefs head-on and transform his mindset from self-doubt to embracing opportunities and growth. Rahul embarks on an exciting journey of self-discovery and empowerment, fuelled by the unwavering support and guidance of his coach. As he progresses, he starts breaking free from the chains of fear and insecurity that once held him captive.

With the guidance of his coach, Rahul discovers the root causes of his limiting beliefs and develops strategies to conquer them. Through self-reflection and introspection, he gains a deeper understanding of his abilities, weaknesses, and areas for growth. Rahul's confidence and motivation skyrocket as he continues to attend coaching sessions, propelling him closer to his dream of starting his own business.

As Rahul charges ahead with his ambitious plan to start his own company, he faces a series of challenges and setbacks along the way. With an unwavering sense of resilience and a growth mindset, he fearlessly tackles every obstacle that comes his way. Each challenge he conquers becomes a stepping stone to his personal growth and strength.

Rahul's unwavering determination and the unwavering support of his coach propelled him towards his dreams of becoming an entrepreneur. With sheer grit and perseverance, he triumphantly launched his own business, achieving his long-awaited objectives. **Witness the incredible power of coaching to shatter limiting beliefs and unleash the untapped potential within every person. This individual's journey serves as undeniable proof of the profound impact coaching can have.**

Call for Action: Contemplate your own limiting beliefs and to think about the ways in which coaching principles can enable you to break free from the restrictions of fear and self-doubt.

This will ultimately lead to the realization of your fullest potential and the accomplishment of your dreams.

3.3 Discovery Exercise: identifying the limiting beliefs.

Start on a journey of self-discovery by identifying the limiting beliefs that may be preventing you from making progress toward your goals and aspirations. When it comes to confronting and overcoming the internal obstacles that stand in the way of personal development and fulfilment, this exercise serves as an important first step that everyone should do.

Step 1: Make room for introspection: Set aside specific time and space for the purpose of contemplation.

Step 2: Identifying areas of discomfort. Consider the aspects of your life in which you are experiencing feelings of stagnation or dissatisfaction. In any other element of your life, where you might be facing resistance or self-doubt, these could be related to your work goals, relationships, personal development, or any other aspect of your existence.

Step 3: investigate the origins of beliefs: Investigate the places where your limiting ideas originated. It is possible that these ideas are the result of previous experiences, societal training, the expectations of one's family, or cultural conventions.

Step 4: Do these beliefs have a foundation in objective reality, or are they only founded on assumptions or interpretations of experiences that have occurred in earlier times?

Challenge the evidence that supports these ideas and to investigate alternate points of view.

Step 5: Consider the ways in which your limiting beliefs have impacted your ideas, feelings, and behaviours. Do you find that these ideas have resulted in behaviours that are self-defeating, opportunities that have been missed, or feelings of inadequacy?

Step 6: Develop Beliefs That Affirm Your Capabilities: Create ideas that are powerful and align with your value system and objectives. Affirmations, exercises in visualization, or the search for positive role models and mentors who exemplify the beliefs and values that they aspire to acquire are all examples of activities that could be included in this category.

When you fully engage in the process of uncovering your limiting beliefs, you open yourself up to gaining a clear understanding of the internal obstacles that might be holding you back from achieving your goals and aspirations. Once you grasp this valuable insight, you can start to question and surpass these beliefs, opening the door to personal growth, strength, and a renewed feeling of empowerment.

Chapters 1, 2, and 3 combine to create a cohesive story of human growth and change. These themes of self-discovery, passion exploration, and overcoming limiting beliefs are all interconnected, creating an exciting journey of growth and transformation. Get ready to embark on an incredible journey of self-discovery and empowerment! This book will take you on a thrilling adventure where you'll uncover your true potential, face challenges head-on, and break free from any limitations you've placed on yourself. Get ready to embark on an incredible journey of self-discovery and empowerment! You'll be equipped with all the resources, insights, and motivation you need to unlock your full potential and create a life filled with purpose, fulfilment, and joy. It's time to unleash your inner greatness and embrace the amazing adventure that lies ahead!

4.Embracing Authenticity: Finding Strength in Vulnerability

Personal growth thrives when individuals embrace their true selves and live in alignment with their own ideas and goals. It's all about being authentic and staying true to oneself.

Welcome aboard as we embark on the thrilling fourth chapter of our incredible journey! We're thrilled to have you join us and can't wait to see what lies ahead. Get ready to dive into the exciting world of personal development and connection as we explore the powerful impact of honesty and vulnerability in this chapter! In this chapter titled "Embracing Authenticity: Finding Strength in Vulnerability," we explore the incredible power of accepting our true selves and embracing vulnerability. By doing so, we open ourselves up to deeper connections, a greater sense of fulfilment, and a truly authentic way of living.

In the fourth chapter, we dive deeper into personal development and transformation, building upon the concepts introduced in the previous chapters. Get ready to expand your knowledge and take your growth to the next level! Get ready to dive into the exciting discoveries we made during our investigation in this chapter! In the first chapter, titled "The Power of Coaching Miracles," we explored the incredible impact of coaching on individuals, helping them unlock their true potential and find empowerment through self-discovery. In the second chapter, titled "Discovering Potential: Unleashing the Power Within," we urged you to uncover their inherent abilities and unique qualities. In the third chapter, titled "Breaking Barriers: Overcoming Limiting Beliefs," we dive into the internal obstacles that often hinder personal growth.

Now that we've reached Chapter 4, let's dive into the importance of authenticity and vulnerability when it comes to understanding our own identity. Personal growth thrives when individuals embrace their true selves and live in alignment with their own ideas and goals. It's all about being authentic and staying true to oneself. It's amazing how we can develop such meaningful connections with ourselves and others. These connections allow us to grow in empathy, compassion, and sincerity. In order to reach this objective, you have to embrace vulnerability with open arms.

In this chapter, we aim to ignite your curiosity and encourage you to delve into the concepts of authenticity and vulnerability. By exploring these characteristics and their impact on your life and relationships, we hope to inspire you to embark on a journey of self-discovery.

4.1 Illustration with Example

Let's dive into the incredible **story of Mahatma Gandhi**, a true inspiration for leadership and social change. We'll explore how his honesty and vulnerability transformed the world.

Mahatma Gandhi's incredible journey is a shining testament to his unwavering dedication to truth and sincerity, even in the face of immense opposition and adversity. His commitment was evident in every aspect of his life. Gandhi's unwavering commitment to his ideas and principles remained steadfast, even in the face of formidable obstacles presented by colonial power and social injustice. He skilfully guided with a genuine and heartfelt approach.

From the very beginning, Gandhi displayed an incredible fearlessness in embracing vulnerability and fearlessly speaking the truth to those in power, regardless of the risks it posed to his own safety. His unwavering commitment to nonviolent resistance and civil disobedience ignited a global movement for justice and equality, inspiring millions to join the fight for India's independence and sparking similar movements worldwide.

Gandhi's actions, words, and unwavering dedication to the pursuit of truth and justice showcased his authenticity and openness. He exuded a rare combination of honesty and vulnerability. Through his simple and humble lifestyle, he inspired others to join him in building a more compassionate and just society.

Gandhi stayed true to his values and principles, never wavering in his integrity or his dedication to nonviolence, even in the face of imprisonment, brutality, and attempts on his life. His unwavering determination to embrace vulnerability and overcome suffering made him a true inspiration to countless individuals, both in India and beyond its borders.

4.Embracing Authenticity

Gandhi's authenticity and openness played a vital role in India's struggle for independence. They played a crucial role in sparking massive movements and rallying everyday individuals to stand up against injustice. The powerful impact he made continues to inspire future leaders and activists to lead with integrity, genuineness, and a commitment to speaking truth to those in positions of power.

Call for Action: Contemplate your own personal journey of authenticity and vulnerability.

You can begin to foster a greater sense of honesty and vulnerability by engaging in self-reflection and becoming more self-aware. This can pave the way for personal development, connection, and social transformation.

4.2 Real life Case Study

Maya, a vibrant young professional who is on a quest to express her true self in all aspects of her life, is embarking on an incredible journey of self-discovery, and together, we will delve into every step of this transformative adventure. Coaching can empower individuals to embrace their true selves and embrace their vulnerability, resulting in stronger connections and increased happiness. Maya's story is a powerful example of how coaching can truly empower individuals.

As Maya embarks on her thrilling adventure, she finds herself caught in a constant state of disconnection and discontentment. Although Maya seems to be thriving in her work, she is grappling with a deep feeling of emptiness and solitude. She struggles to convey her true self and establish deep connections with others. Maya hesitates to express her true thoughts and emotions in her professional life due to her fear of being judged or rejected. In her professional life, she exudes an air of competence and professionalism, always wearing a mask that never falters. Maya struggles to open up and show her vulnerable side to others in her personal life. She fosters relationships that are shallow and often feels lonely as a consequence.

In this pivotal moment, Maya decides to consult a coach to enhance her performance. Maya embarks on an exciting journey of self-discovery and empowerment through the transformative process of coaching. She embraces her honesty and vulnerability as powerful assets instead of seeing them as weaknesses. Maya is finally shedding the layers that have kept her disconnected from herself and others. It's an exciting journey of self-discovery! Her coach is giving her a boost of energy and motivation as she navigates through this process.

Through self-reflection and introspection, Maya gains a deeper understanding of her true self, including her values, passions, and goals. She discovers the power to confront and overcome the thoughts and fears that have held her back from fully embracing her true self, as she becomes adept at recognizing and addressing them head-on. Maya realizes that embracing vulnerability is a powerful display of her humanity and bravery as she navigates through each coaching session. She embraces vulnerability and becomes more at ease with it.

4.Embracing Authenticity

As Maya embarks on a new chapter in her life, she undergoes a remarkable change in her relationships and overall happiness. It's an exciting time of growth and self-discovery for her. Maya's newfound authenticity and vulnerability in her professional life allows her to form deeper connections with her co-workers and clients, fostering trust and collaboration. Maya's openness to vulnerability in her personal life leads to deeper connections and closeness in her relationships, ultimately bringing greater satisfaction and a sense of achievement.

Maya's incredible journey of embracing honesty and vulnerability leads to a profound sense of empowerment and meaning in her life. That's what she's striving for on her journey. **Maya learns a valuable lesson during her coaching journey - that real strength lies in embracing her authentic self, flaws and all, and being open to being seen and valued for who she truly is.**

Call for Action: contemplate your own journey of authenticity and vulnerability. What are some ways that you might use Maya's example to motivate yourself to accept who you truly are and to build stronger connections in your own life?

You can begin to peel aside the layers of self-protection and pretence that keep you detached from yourself and others by engaging in introspection and cultivating self-awareness. This will pave the way for greater authenticity, fulfilment, and connection.

4.3 Discovery Exercise: self-reflection as a means of investigating

Participate in self-reflection as a means of investigating moments in your life when your felt the most authentic and vulnerable.

Step 1: Remember genuine moments: Think back to particular instances in your life when you had a sense of authenticity.

Step 2: Investigate the Vulnerability: Reflect on instances in which you experienced feelings of vulnerability. Think about the feelings that you experienced during these times, such as fear, uncertainty, courage, or acceptance, and how these feelings impacted your conduct and how you interacted with other people.

Step 3: Investigate the Connections: Think about the ways in which you connected with other people during these genuine and intimate times. During your interactions with other people, did you feel a sense of intimacy, empathy, or understanding?

Step 4: Acquire New Perspectives: Think on the insights you have obtained from events like these. In what ways did you expand your understanding of yourself, your beliefs, and the connections you had? What are some examples of lessons that can be transferred to future experiences and interactions?

Step 5: Incorporate thankfulness: Incorporate thankfulness into your daily life, thanks to these instances of authenticity and vulnerability.

Expressing gratitude for these events can help cultivate a deeper sense of self-awareness and appreciation for the richness of human connection. These encounters are crucial and meaningful in your journey towards personal growth!

I urge you to embrace your own personal journey of authenticity and vulnerability with enthusiasm! How do these characteristics shape your life and the way they interact with others? What factors prevent individuals from fully embracing your true selves and being more open and vulnerable? By taking the time to reflect on ourselves and increase our self-awareness, we can cultivate a stronger connection to honesty and vulnerability. It's an exciting journey that you can embark on to discover your true self. Get ready to unlock a world of meaningful connections, personal growth, and pure contentment!

With an electrifying energy, we embark on a transformative journey of self-discovery and empowerment in Chapter 4, the starting point of our quest for a more meaningful and authentic way of living. Authenticity and vulnerability will be our guiding lights along this path.

5.Navigating Challenges: Building Resilience in the Face of Adversity

Embracing self-discovery, authenticity, and vulnerability qualities is absolutely crucial for building resilience in the face of adversity.

In Chapter 5, "Navigating Challenges: Building Resilience in the Face of Adversity," we explore the crucial skill of resilience and how it helps us overcome obstacles and setbacks on our path to personal growth and transformation. Our main focus is on the impact of resilience in bouncing back from adversity. Let's dive into it! This chapter expands on the foundational concepts introduced in the preceding chapters, offering valuable strategies and perspectives for effectively navigating life's challenges with resilience and determination.

In Chapter 5, we bring together the exciting ideas of coaching, self-discovery, authenticity, and vulnerability. These concepts are intertwined as we navigate challenges and cultivate resilience. Get ready for an exciting continuation of the themes we explored in the previous chapters! In Chapter 5, it is emphasized that embracing these qualities is absolutely crucial for building resilience in the face of adversity. Remember when we talked about the amazing power of authenticity and vulnerability in Chapter 4? Well, this is just like that!

In this chapter, I invite you to explore the idea of resilience and consider how you can cultivate this essential skill to overcome the obstacles and setbacks you face in life. As we explore the mindset and strategies that empower people to bounce back from challenges and come out even stronger, we bring in real-life stories, case studies, and hands-on activities.

5.1 Illustration with example

For the purpose of demonstrating the transformative force of perseverance and determination in overcoming adversity and driving social change, we draw inspiration from the incredible narrative of Nelson Mandela.

It is a credit to **Nelson Mandela**'s amazing resilience and tenacity that he was able to endure decades of imprisonment and tyranny during the apartheid system in South Africa. His journey is a testament to this extraordinary resilience and perseverance. In spite of the insurmountable challenges he faced and the fact that he was held in solitary confinement for a period of 27 years, Nelson Mandela never wavered in his dedication to the cause of justice, equality, and the fight against apartheid.

Mandela was able to keep his dignity, courage, and unshakeable confidence in the inherent value and dignity of every individual throughout his whole time spent in jail. Because of his ability to persevere in the face of suffering, he became a symbol of hope for millions of oppressed people in South Africa and around the world, motivating them to keep fighting for freedom and equality.

Mandela's perseverance was not simply an acceptance of his circumstances in a passive manner; rather, it was a proactive commitment to bring about change and to create a better future for his people. Mandela continued to struggle for the rights of all South Africans even while he was held in prison. He engaged in negotiations with the administration that maintained apartheid and laid the framework for a peaceful transition to democracy.

When Nelson Mandela was released from jail in 1994, he became a symbol of hope and peace, and he led South Africa into a new era of democracy and healing. In spite of the enormous difficulties that the nation was experiencing, Nelson Mandela remained steadfast in his dedication to constructing a society that was founded on justice, equality, and reconciliation rather than vengeance or retribution.

Not only did Mandela's leadership during this crucial period illustrate his ability to persevere in the face of hardship, but it also demonstrated his capacity to motivate people to triumph over their own obstacles and work toward a shared vision of a better future. As a result of his leadership, Nelson Mandela was able to bring together a nation that was terribly divided and establish a model of forgiveness and reconciliation that continues to reverberate around the world

---

Call for Action: Contemplate your own experiences of adversity and to think about ways in which you might nurture resilience in your life. What are some ways that you might harness the power of Mandela's example to triumph over challenges and emerge more powerful?

> Create the mentality and abilities necessary to navigate the problems that life presents with confidence, fortitude, and resolve by engaging in periods of reflection and increasing YOUR awareness of yourself.

1.2 Real life Case study

Shashank's story is a powerful example of how individuals can conquer challenges and achieve great success.

Shashank, being a young entrepreneur, has experienced numerous business setbacks. Shashank is confronted with market changes, finance concerns, and competition, even though he started off with great enthusiasm and put in a lot of hard work. Shashank's confidence wavers with every setback, causing him to question his abilities as an entrepreneur.

Shashank builds resilience by embracing setbacks as valuable learning experiences with the help of coaching and mentoring. His coach encourages him to view failures as valuable lessons that can propel his entrepreneurial career forward. Shashank's growth mindset enables him to view challenges as opportunities for growth, empowering him to conquer them.

Shashank's journey towards building resilience involves embracing the lessons learned from his mistakes. Shashank is eager to receive constructive feedback and engage in self-reflection in order to evolve and improve his approach, rather than fixating on past setbacks. Shashank's commitment to constant learning and progress fuels his personal and professional growth, as he embraces failures as opportunities for improvement.

Shashank continues to pursue his commercial endeavours with unwavering determination, even in the face of numerous challenges. Shashank faces every challenge with unwavering determination and unwavering belief. He harnesses his setbacks to drive his entrepreneurial journey.

Shashank's unwavering determination enables him to navigate the unpredictable journey of entrepreneurship with ease. Shashank's unwavering determination and eagerness to learn from his mess ups propel him past obstacles, build momentum, and achieve triumph in his endeavours. **Shashank is truly driven by his passion and has a strong desire to make a positive impact on the world through his entrepreneurial endeavours.**

> Call for Action: Examine your own struggles. How have you handled life challenges? How have you built resilience and persevered?
>
> Introspection and self-awareness can help you develop the mindset and abilities needed to overcome life's problems with strength, courage, and tenacity, leading to success and fulfilment.

Shashank's journey towards building resilience has been greatly supported by coaching.

Coaching as a Resilient Catalyst: Shashank thrives with the help of coaching, which provides valuable assistance and support during his entrepreneurial setbacks. Coaching provides Shashank with a secure space to analyse his setbacks, reconsider his perspectives, and create strategies to conquer them.

Shashank embraces setbacks as valuable learning opportunities through coaching, which promotes continuous learning and personal growth. His coach motivates him to embrace his failures as opportunities for growth and use them to fuel his future success. Shashank's resilience gets a boost as he adapts and improves through reflective learning.

Shashank's coach provides guidance, valuable insights, and a strong sense of accountability. Shashank's coach is always there to support him and push him to take action towards his goals, even when things get tough. Shashank's ability to overcome setbacks is fuelled by a combination of accountability and support.

Shashank's self-efficacy and confidence soar as he embraces coaching and discovers his true potential to tackle any problem. Shashank's incredible growth and numerous triumphs, fuelled by his unwavering belief in his own abilities, serve as a testament to his resilience in the face of adversity. Shashank's growing confidence is fuelling his resilience.

With the integration of resilience-building techniques, the coaching approach empowers Shashank to develop personalized strategies and access valuable resources to effectively navigate through challenges. Shashank incorporates various resilience-building techniques into his daily routine, following his coach's guidance. These techniques range from practicing mindfulness to engaging in strengths-based reflection.

Ultimately, coaching empowers Shashank to build resilience by providing guidance, encouragement, and access to necessary tools, enabling him to tackle challenges with unwavering resolve. Shashank's journey is filled with challenges, but with the guidance of his coach, he emerges stronger and more resilient. This newfound strength propels him towards entrepreneurial success and a deep sense of fulfilment.

5.3 Discovery Exercise: Adversity Journal

For fortitude and perspective on life's challenges, you are recommended to keep an Adversity Journal.

Purpose of Adversity Journal: You can record your adversity experiences, reflect on the lessons learned, and chart your personal growth in the Adversity Journal. Write about your problems and insights to better understand your resilience-building journey and develop perspective and resilience for future situations.

Starting an Adversity Journal:

Step 1: Choose a diary or notebook you enjoy writing in. A physical journal or digital platform must be easy to use and accessible.

Step 2: Set aside daily, weekly, or monthly time for thought. This period lets you revisit your challenges, reflect on your answers, and find patterns and insights.

Step 3: Record Adversity: Journal your hardship, including challenges, feelings, and coping mechanisms.

Step 4: Think on the lessons and insights you obtained from each setback. What did you discover about your strengths and coping mechanisms? How did the event change you?
Step 5: Track own Growth: Utilize the Adversity Journal to track your own development. Encourage you to look for patterns in your adversity reactions and celebrate your improvement and resilience as you review earlier postings.

The Adversity Journal helps you build resilience, perspective, and personal growth in the face of life's hardships. You can build resilience and strength to handle adversity by reflecting on your experiences and thoughts

In the fifth chapter, we set out on a journey to create resilience by investigating the mentality and methods that enable individuals to recover from hardship and emerge more powerful than you were before. Come along with us as we explore the transformational power of resilience and learn how to face the challenges that life throws at you with strength, courage, and determination.

6. Empowering Dreams: Turning Vision into Reality

Resilience remains crucial for achieving our goals, even in the face of challenges and setbacks.

Turning Vision into Reality," takes you on an exhilarating journey of transformation. It explores how individuals can tap into their aspirations and ambitions to create meaningful change in their lives and the world. Get ready for an exhilarating journey as we embark on the adventure of transforming dreams into tangible achievements! In this chapter, we dive deeper into the themes that were introduced earlier. You'll find a wealth of insights and practical tactics that will help you pursue and achieve your aspirations with gusto!

Get ready for an exhilarating chapter where we explore the powerful concepts of resiliency, authenticity, and self-discovery, all within the exciting framework of pursuing your dreams and aspirations! Get ready for an exciting continuation of the themes we explored in the previous chapters! In Chapter 5, we explored the importance of resilience in overcoming barriers. Now, in Chapter 6, we see that resilience remains crucial for achieving our goals, even in the face of challenges and setbacks.

Hey there! In this chapter, I'm super excited to inspire you to explore the amazing power of dreams and aspirations in shaping your personal growth and transformation. Let's dive in and discover the incredible potential you hold! Let's dive into the mindset and strategies that empower people to clarify their vision, set goals, and take decisive action to achieve their ambitions! Through the incorporation of real-life examples, case studies, and engaging practical activities, we are able to achieve this.

6.1 Illustration with example

Using patience, tenacity, and unshakable commitment, the tale of **APJ Abdul Kalam offers as a powerful illustration of how anyone may make their aspirations come true via the application of these very same qualities.**

As a child, APJ Abdul Kalam had an ambition of becoming a pilot. This dream continued throughout his life. In spite of the fact that Kalam came from a humble family and had to contend with financial restraints, his dream served as a source of motivation and spurred him to triumph over a multitude of challenges in order to achieve his objective. When Kalam was growing up in Rameswaram, a tiny town in Tamil Nadu, his dream of flying high appeared impossible to achieve due to the low means that his family had and the expectations that society had of him. In this particular scenario, coaching could have been an important factor in providing Kalam with the necessary support, direction, and encouragement he needs in order to maintain his concentration on his objectives and triumph over challenges that he encountered along the road.

However, despite the fact that the odds were stacked against him, Kalam did not waver in his determination to pursue his dream. Throughout his academic career, he was a dedicated student who excelled in his studies and demonstrated a strong interest in the fields of science and technology. In spite of the fact that he was experiencing financial difficulties, Kalam remained resolute in his determination to forge his own way and reject the expectations of society that defined his future.

Kalam's desire of becoming a pilot evolved into a more expansive aspiration to make a contribution to the disciplines of science and technology as a result of his hard work, tenacity, and unrelenting pursuit of perfection. After earning a degree in aerospace engineering, he went on to become a member of India's missile program, where he made important contributions to the nation's defence capabilities.

It is a monument to the transformative power of dreams that Kalam went from being a little lad from a tiny village with a dream to becoming one of the most revered and respected leaders in India. Kalam exemplified the principles of honesty, humility, and service to humanity, despite the fact that he achieved success in the world of science and technology. He remained humble and grounded throughout his incredible career.

Kalam was able to motivate millions of individuals over his whole life by virtue of his vision, leadership, and unyielding dedication to exceptional performance. He inspired young people to have lofty aspirations, to formulate lofty objectives, and to work diligently in order to accomplish them. His legacy continues to motivate people all across the world, including generations of Indians, to pursue their aspirations with the same level of fervour, perseverance, and tenacity that you had when you were young.

The tale of APJ Abdul Kalam offers as a powerful illustration of how individuals may convert their aspirations into reality through the application of tenacity, perseverance, and unshakable commitment. This chapter focuses on the necessity of having a clear vision, making goals, and taking decisive action in order to follow one's dreams. The path of empowerment and change that Kalam has taken is a perfect example of the ideas that are discussed in this chapter. In the same way that Kalam's childhood dream of becoming a pilot became the spark that ignited his passion and led him to accomplish greatness, you are urged to reflect on your own hopes and aspirations and contemplate how you might convert your vision into reality through inspired action and steadfast dedication.

> Call for Action: Think about how you can pursue your desires and goals with the same level of commitment and tenacity. You are encouraged to clarify your vision, establish significant goals, and take decisive action in order to create the life of your dreams.
>
> This is accomplished through introspection and self-awareness.

6.2 Real life Case study

Let me tell you about **Ayesha, a dynamic young entrepreneur with a burning passion for launching her own sustainable fashion line.** Her story is a powerful example of the incredible transformation that individuals undergo to turn their dreams into tangible success. Ayesha's story highlights the importance of never giving up and staying determined. It also underscores the crucial role that coaching and mentoring play in guiding individuals towards their goals and objectives.

Feel free to explore the potential of your dreams and goals to create real change. Through the narrative of Ayesha, you'll witness the practical application of concepts like defining your vision, establishing your goals, and taking decisive action to turn your dreams into reality. It's an inspiring journey!

Ayesha greatly benefits from the guidance and assistance she receives through mentoring and coaching, which plays a crucial role in her journey. With a clear vision and a strategic roadmap, she navigates the complexities of entrepreneurship and achieves her goals. These guiding influences empower her to negotiate and clarify her path to success. As Ayesha works towards gaining clarity on her target audience, refining her company model, and aligning her principles with her entrepreneurial pursuits, she is fortunate to receive guidance from her coach and mentor.

Despite facing challenges like limited funds and supply chain difficulties, Ayesha remains unwavering in her determination to pursue her dream. Her unwavering faith in the power of her vision and her unwavering commitment to sustainability have allowed her to overcome challenges with unwavering determination. Ayesha is able to pursue her goals with unwavering determination, fuelled by her deep passion and the unwavering support of her community. She tackles challenges head-on and refuses to back down.

Over time, Ayesha's unwavering determination and unwavering commitment pay off with concrete results - she achieves her dream of launching an environmentally conscious fashion line! With her strategic planning, innovative thinking, and unwavering determination, **Ayesha consistently achieves her entrepreneurial goals and makes a positive impact on both the fashion industry and the environment. Her achievements showcase the incredible potential of dreams and the profound influence that individuals can have when you wholeheartedly pursue your passions.**

Call for Action: Focus on your own ideas and aspirations and to take aggressive actions toward accomplishing them by reading Ayesha's tale, which acts as a source of inspiration for you.

The narrative of Ayesha gives us the ability to harness your passions, seek help when it is necessary, and persevere in the face of adversity as you strive towards your own aspirations. This is accomplished by presenting the transforming journey from vision to reality.

6.3 Discovery Exercise: Visual Dashboard

You are encouraged to start on a creative journey of self-discovery and goal-setting. This journey may be a highly rewarding experience. This powerful tool acts as a tangible depiction of your hopes and aspirations, providing you with a visual reminder of your objectives and pushing upi to take action in order to bring your wants into physical reality.

You are able to bring your goals to life in a way that is both concrete and visually engaging through the use of the vision board, which serves as a strong visualization tool.

Instructions on How to Make a Vision Board:

Step 1: collect resources such as periodicals, newspapers, images, quotes, and art tools.

Step 2: With the help of these resources, construct your vision board, which will enable you to compile a collection of pictures and words that are reflective of your hopes and ambitions.

Step 3: Be particular and identify goals that have a strong resonance with your values and interests.

Step 4: Create and organize: Once you have a collection of images and words at your disposal, you can begin to organize them on a board or poster, so creating a visually pleasing collage that conveys the essence of your thoughts and feelings around your dreams.

6.Empowering Dreams

Step 5: show and Reflect: show it in a prominent location where you will see it many times a day, such as in your bedroom or at your place of employment. Spend a few minutes out of each day to dwell on your vision board, imagining themselves accomplishing your objectives and reaffirming your determination to pursue your desires.

you can improve your ability to envisage achievement and bring your desires into reality by constructing a visual image of your dreams and aspirations within your own minds.
 The vision board acts as a constant source of motivation and inspiration, reminding you of your goals and motivating them to take consistent action towards reaching them.

You can build a positive mindset and reinforce your belief in your potential to achieve success. This is an example of positive reinforcement.

The vision board is a strong tool that enables you to picture your dreams, strengthen your commitment to following your aspirations, and take decisive action toward turning your vision into reality.

6.4 Discovery Exercise: Goal Setting

Setting goals is all about turning your dreams into achievable milestones!

You, who utilize the SMART framework, can set clear and achievable goals that align with your vision and drive you towards success. This framework, which stands for specific, measurable, attainable, relevant, and time-bound, empowers individuals to establish goals that are crystal clear and within reach.

Let's empower you to clearly express your goals by motivating you to provide specific details. When setting goals, it's crucial to be specific and understand the reasons behind them. Encourage individuals to clearly define what you want to achieve and why it matters to you. Specific goals provide the answers to the questions of "What?" and "Why?" Who's there? Where can I find it, and which one should I choose?

It's important to set goals that you can measure, allowing you to track your progress and evaluate your performance over time. You should be motivated to establish specific criteria for tracking your progress towards each goal. Setting achievable goals helps answer the question, "How much?" Alright, let's get right to it! How many are we talking about? So, how can you know when it's finally done?

It's crucial to set goals that are practical and achievable within the given time frame, resources, and strengths. When it comes to setting objectives, it's crucial to inspire you to consider your current circumstances and talents. By setting challenging yet achievable goals, we can ensure success. Attainable goals provide the answer to the question of whether it's possible to achieve this goal with the available resources.

For goals to truly matter, you must align with the values, interests, and long-term aspirations of you. It's all about staying relevant and connected! It's important to make sure that the goals you set for yourself are truly meaningful and worth pursuing. So, I urge you to take a moment and assess how each objective aligns with your overall vision for your life. This will help you prioritize and focus on what truly matters to you. Relevant goals are the key to answering the question, "Does this goal align with my values and long-term objectives?" You hold the answer you're looking for!

You should feel a strong sense of urgency and responsibility when it comes to achieving you goals. It's important to set specific deadlines to ensure timely completion. It's important to motivate you to set realistic timelines for achieving your goals and to break those goals down into smaller, achievable milestones. Time-bound goals give us a clear answer to the question, "When can we achieve this goal?"

Steps to Take in Order to Begin Setting Goals:

Step 1: Reflect on your dreams and objectives, selecting the primary areas in which you want to concentrate your efforts and the goals that you want to accomplish in each of those areas.

Step 2: Identify particular goals by using the SMART criteria. As an illustration, rather than establishing a general objective such as "improving fitness," you should urge them to establish a more particular objective such as "running a half-marathon in six months."

Step 3: Break those goals down into smaller actions that may be taken. By doing so, the goals become more reasonable and attainable, thereby giving a clear roadmap for progress toward achievement.

Step 4: Establish Deadlines: set deadlines for each goal and the action activities that are related with it.

Step 5: Monitor Your Progress and Make Adjustments as Necessary: Monitor your progress toward each objective and to make adjustments to your plans as required.

The process of goal setting through the utilization of the SMART framework gives you the ability to translate your ambitions and objectives into plans that can be implemented and attainable milestones.

Discover your vision and set meaningful goals that resonate with your passions and values. Take a moment to reflect on yourself and gain self-awareness. It's time to unleash your potential! You can easily pinpoint the necessary steps to turn your vision into reality and create a solid action plan to achieve your goals by reflecting on your own hopes and aspirations and drawing conclusions from those reflections. Whether it's starting a business, pursuing a creative endeavour, or making a positive impact in your community, you have the power to take bold action and create the life you've always dreamed of.

Embracing a Passionate and Purposeful Role: you can unlock your true potential and build a life that aligns with your deepest values and desires by wholeheartedly pursuing you passions and goals with determination and perseverance. Embark on an exhilarating journey of self-discovery and empowerment in Chapter 6, where you are invited to unlock your full potential and experience personal growth and fulfilment. Embarking on this path will enable individuals to tap into the incredible potential of your dreams, creating a better tomorrow not only for yourself but also for the people in your lives.

In Chapter 6, you'll find an exciting road map that will guide you towards turning your ambitions into reality. It's all about self-reflection, setting goals, and taking decisive action. Get ready to embark on an incredible journey! When you draw inspiration from the tales of individuals like APJ Abdul Kalam and Ayesha, you are empowered to clarify your vision, establish relevant goals, and pursue your passions with courage and conviction. Get ready to tap into your full potential and create a life that's bursting with purpose, passion, and fulfilment! Join me on an incredible journey of self-discovery and empowerment as we dive into the transformative insights of Chapter 6. Experience the incredible potential of dreams and unlock the ability to turn our visions into reality by joining us on an exciting journey into the power of dreams.

7.Cultivating Confidence: Stepping Into Your Power

Embrace the transformational power of confidence and live a life defined by purpose, passion, and fulfilment!

Welcome to Chapter 7 of our exciting journey toward transformation! Today, we're diving into the incredible power of self-assurance and how it can help us achieve our goals and desires. Get ready for an exhilarating exploration! Come and discover the incredible power of self-assurance in transforming your ability to tackle challenges, seize opportunities, and ultimately build a life filled with purpose and happiness. Welcome to this exciting chapter titled "Cultivating Confidence: Stepping Into Your Power!" Get ready to embark on a journey of self-discovery and growth as we explore how to unleash your inner confidence. Are you ready to take the first step? Let's dive in!

As we dive into our investigation, we'll draw inspiration from individuals who have shown unwavering confidence in the face of challenges, highlighting the incredible power of self-belief. These incredible individuals, from celebrated athletes to trailblazing entrepreneurs, are a constant source of inspiration. They remind us that confidence is not just a trait, but an attitude that can be cultivated and nurtured.

7.Cultivating Confidence

As we move forward in this chapter, we'll dive deeper into a wide range of exercises and tactics that will help you boost your self-confidence from within. If you're ready to make big moves towards your goals and unlock your full potential, building confidence will give you the power to do just that! It holds true whether you're aiming to launch a business, pursue a creative passion, or embark on a fresh adventure.

Get ready to unleash your full potential! I'm here to show you how to banish self-doubt, embrace your amazing abilities, and step into your power with unwavering confidence. It's all about diving deep into introspection, reflecting on your past experiences, and taking actionable steps that will truly make a difference in your life. Embrace the transformational power of confidence and live a life defined by purpose, passion, and fulfilment! Get ready to unlock a world of possibilities, break through any obstacles, and pave your way to success!

Come join us on an exhilarating journey of self-discovery and empowerment! Together, we'll explore the endless possibilities that arise when you embrace confidence and fearlessly step into your own power. Let's harness the incredible power of self-belief and unlock a future bursting with endless possibilities and chances for professional growth!

In earlier chapters, especially Chapter 6, we laid the groundwork for you to explore your ideas and aspirations and start taking concrete steps towards turning your vision into a reality! Chapter 7 expands upon the groundwork established in previous chapters. Having confidence is crucial in this process as it empowers individuals to overcome challenges, make calculated risks, and pursue their goals with unwavering determination.

Get ready to dive into this chapter and explore the incredible impact that confidence can have on your life. Discover strategies for building and nurturing your own self-assurance that will stay with you for years to come! Throughout the course of the book, you'll find real-life examples, practical activities, and introspective reflections that will help you unlock your inner confidence and step into your power. Get ready to discover the keys to unleashing your full potential!

7.1 Illustration with example

The story of **Serena Williams** is a powerful example of how unwavering self-confidence and belief in oneself can create a remarkable transformation. Throughout her remarkable tennis journey, Williams faced numerous challenges and setbacks, such as injuries, criticism, and even discrimination. But what set her apart was her unshakeable confidence and determination to succeed, even in the face of opposition.

Even with obstacles on and off the court, Serena Williams never let anything dim her self-confidence and abilities. Williams always maintained an unwavering belief in her own greatness, never letting injuries, tough opponents, or criticism from naysayers shake her determination. With unwavering confidence, she fearlessly tackled obstacles, using her determination and persistence to come out victorious.

7.Cultivating Confidence

Williams' incredible journey from a young girl with a goal to becoming one of the greatest athletes of all time has inspired countless people worldwide to believe in themselves and chase their dreams. Her life story is an incredible example of how having confidence in oneself and believing in one's abilities can lead to extraordinary achievements and reaching one's true potential. Williams has shown that with confidence and determination, one can achieve anything they put their mind to. He has accomplished this by consistently defying limitations and bouncing back from obstacles.

Serena Williams has had the privilege of working with exceptional coaches who have played a crucial role in shaping her career. These coaches have provided invaluable guidance, helping her refine her skills, strengthen her mindset, and conquer challenges along the way. These coaches have provided her with invaluable support. Williams's achievement is truly remarkable, and it's clear that her innate skill and unrelenting work ethic were key factors in her success. Williams has received invaluable feedback, techniques, and encouragement from her coaches, which have helped her build the confidence and resilience needed to perform at her absolute best.

Let me tell you, the story of Serena Williams is absolutely mind-blowing! It's a **powerful reminder of how self-belief and confidence can truly transform someone and help them achieve incredible accomplishments. Williams has been a true inspiration to countless individuals worldwide, motivating them to chase their dreams with**

unwavering determination, resilience, and self-confidence.

Call for Action: Nurture your own confidence and belief in yourself as you reflect on Williams' tale within the context of Chapter 7.

If you have the appropriate mindset and are determined, you too are capable of overcoming challenges and accomplishing your objectives.

7.2 Real Life Case study

The journey of **Raj, from self-doubt to the success of his entrepreneurial endeavours**

Raj's tale offers as an illuminating illustration of how individuals can triumph over self-doubt and fear in order to follow their aspirations with confidence and conviction. Raj, who has recently graduated from college and has the goal of launching his own company, struggles with emotions of uncertainty and uneasiness, and he questions his capacity to be successful in the highly competitive world of entrepreneurship. In spite of this, Raj goes on a transforming journey of self-discovery and empowerment with the assistance of coaching and mentorship. As a result, he ultimately realizes his entrepreneurial objectives and achieves success that is beyond his wildest expectations.

Raj is tormented by self-doubt and fear of failure in the beginning of his journey. He also harbours limiting beliefs that threaten to prevent him from pursuing his aspirations of becoming an entrepreneur. On the other hand, Raj is able to learn how to confront these ideas with the assistance of his coach and mentor. He comes to the realization that these beliefs are obstacles to his achievement rather than unchangeable realities. Through the process of introspection and reflection, Raj is able to determine the underlying factors that contribute to his feelings of self-doubt. He then begins to reframe his mentality by replacing negative self-talk with affirmations of his talents and feelings of worth.

As Raj continues to delve deeper into his quest of self-discovery, he comes to the realization that he possesses a diverse array of qualities and talents that he had previously neglected to acknowledge. By participating in guided exercises and engaging in self-reflection, Raj acknowledges and appreciates his one-of-a-kind capabilities, talents, and achievements, thereby acknowledging them as sources of strength and resilience. Through the process of recognizing his accomplishments and embracing his abilities, Raj is able to cultivate a fresh feeling of self-assurance and confidence, which in turn lays the groundwork for his future endeavours in the realm of entrepreneurship.

During the course of his journey, Raj is inevitably confronted with a number of obstacles and problems, some of which include unsuccessful commercial endeavours and difficulties in his personal life. Instead of viewing failure as a reflection of his inferiority, Raj learns to embrace it as an opportunity for growth and learning. This allows him to change his perspective on failure. Raj is able to reframe his perception of failure with the assistance of his coach and mentor. He comes to the realization that failure is an inevitable component of the trip on the path to becoming an entrepreneur and that it is a priceless source of learning and insights. Raj is able to become more robust in the face of hardship as a result of this newly acquired viewpoint. He is able to learn from his mistakes and use them as a source of motivation for his continuing growth and development.

As Raj's self-assurance increases, so does his courage to pursue his entrepreneurial goals with wholehearted conviction and unwavering persistence. The newly discovered sense of self-assurance that Raj possesses encourages him to take aggressive steps toward the establishment of his own firm. He does this by capitalizing on his abilities, talents, and experiences in order to bring his vision to life. Raj tackles his enterprise with unflinching confidence and commitment, knowing that he possesses the resiliency and resourcefulness to overcome any hurdle that may come his way. This is in spite of the inherent dangers and uncertainties that are associated with being an entrepreneur.

In the end of his journey, Raj realizes his full potential as an entrepreneur and a leader by launching a successful enterprise, which he has dreamed of doing for a very long time. The unshakeable confidence, resiliency, and dedication that Raj possesses allow him to not only accomplish his objectives but also beyond them, leaving an indelible mark on both his field and the society in which he operates. Others are inspired to pursue their aspirations with courage and conviction as a result of his success, which acts as a witness to the transformational power of self-belief and confidence in oneself.

One of the most important aspects of Raj's journey is the crucial assistance and direction that he receives from his coach and trainer. Raj is able to overcome the obstacles of self-doubt and fear by utilizing their expertise, encouragement, and unwavering conviction in his potential. As a result, he emerges from these experiences more powerful, more self-assured, and more resilient than he was before. **The tremendous difference that supporting advice and mentorship can have in an individual's journey towards success is highlighted by Raj's change from a cautious dreamer to a confident entrepreneur. This metamorphosis is a clear example of the success that can be achieved via coaching.**

<table><tr><td>

Call for Action: Develop your own sense of self-assurance and confidence.

You are filled with the knowledge that, with the appropriate frame of mind and dedication, you, too, are capable of accomplishing your objectives and establishing a life that is filled with purpose, passion, and fulfilment.

</td></tr></table>

7.3 Discovery Exercise: Positive Affirmations

Constructing Your Mindset for Confidence Through the Use of Positive Affirmations

The practice of positive affirmations emerges as a powerful tool to reinforce positive attitudes about yourself and your skills. This affirmation practice is a powerful tool because it allows you to step into your power. By incorporating daily affirmations into your routine, you have the ability to effectively rewire your attitude and create confidence from within, so empowering yourself to pursue your dreams with courage and conviction.

Positive affirmations are statements or phrases that affirm positive views about oneself, one's abilities, and one's potential for success. Positive affirmations can be used in personal development. Individuals are able to combat negative self-talk and replace it with empowering and uplifting ideas that encourage confidence and self-assurance when they frequently repeat these affirmations to themselves. Individuals have the ability to rewire their subconscious mind by performing positive affirmations over and over again, which can result in the development of a more optimistic and empowering mindset.

Incorporate positive affirmations into your daily routine as a form of self-care and self-empowerment. Setting aside specific time to repeat affirmations may be extremely good for the development of self-confidence and self-belief. This can be done for a variety of reasons, including first thing in the morning, before going to bed, or at various points throughout the day.

Some examples of affirmations that are positive:
"I am capable of achieving my goals and dreams."
"I am deserving of success and abundance in all areas of my life."
"I have the courage to pursue my dreams and overcome any obstacle."
"I believe in myself and my abilities to create the life I desire."

"I am resilient, and I bounce back from challenges stronger than ever."
"I embrace failure as a natural part of the learning process and grow from it."
"I trust in my intuition and make decisions with confidence and clarity."
"I am worthy of love, respect, and happiness."
"I am a magnet for opportunities, and I attract success effortlessly."
"I am confident, capable, and unstoppable in the pursuit of my dreams."

Affirmations of positivity have such advantages:

You increase your confidence and self-esteem by affirming positive thoughts about yourself on a frequent basis. The use of positive affirmations can assist in the process of reshaping yours self-perception, enabling individuals to view themselves in a more favourable light and to appreciate the distinctive features and abilities that they possess. Affirmations help develop a mindset that is resilient, which enables you to recover from failures and challenges with a sense of resolve and resilience. You can improve your ability to clarify your vision and remain focused on what genuinely matters to you by concentrating on affirmations that are in alignment with your objectives and aspirations.

In Chapter 7, I encourage you to embark on an exciting journey of self-reflection. It's time to evaluate your current levels of confidence and discover areas where you can cultivate even stronger self-assurance. Get ready to dive deep and discover your true potential! You can gain valuable insights into your strengths, weaknesses, and areas for growth by actively reflecting on yourself and honestly evaluating your progress. By recognizing your successes, celebrating your achievements, and embracing failure as a normal part of the learning journey, you can cultivate a mindset of self-assurance and perseverance that will empower you to fearlessly pursue your goals.

In the earlier chapters, especially Chapter 6, we dove into some exciting topics. We talked about clarifying your vision and setting meaningful goals that align with your dreams and aspirations. These topics are closely connected to what we'll be discussing in Chapter 7. Confidence is absolutely crucial when it comes to achieving our goals. It empowers us to take bold action and conquer any obstacles that come our way. You can uncover areas where you need to focus and develop strategies to boost your self-confidence by reflecting on your vision and goals in relation to your current level of assurance.

Get ready to embark on an exciting journey in this Chapter! It's all about empowering yourself and boosting your confidence as you chase after your dreams and aspirations. Let's dive in and discover the road map that will guide you every step of the way! You'll be empowered to discover your inner confidence, conquer self-doubt, and fully embrace your potential with the help of real-life examples, practical activities, and introspective thoughts. Get ready to unlock your true potential! With an unwavering belief in oneself, You can create a life filled with purpose, passion, and fulfilment. You will have the courage and determination to pursue your goals fearlessly.

8.Creating Connections: Building Supportive Networks

Your network is your Net worth.

Welcome to Chapter 8 of our incredible journey toward transformation! Today, we're going to explore the vital importance of creating meaningful connections and building supportive networks in our lives. Get ready for an exciting and enlightening adventure! Welcome to this exciting chapter titled "Creating Connections: Building Supportive Networks!" In this chapter, we will explore the incredible impact that connections can have on our personal growth, professional success, and overall happiness. Get ready to dive into the world of building meaningful relationships!

Let me tell you, there is nothing quite like the power of connection. I cannot stress enough how important it is to foster meaningful connections in a world that is becoming increasingly interconnected. It's truly remarkable! The connections we form have a powerful effect on shaping our experiences and influencing the results we attain. It holds true in all aspects of our lives, whether we're teaming up with colleagues, learning from seasoned experts, or nurturing meaningful friendships.

Let's dive into the incredible journey of conquering life's challenges together!

Life is full of challenges and uncertainties, but it's in these moments that our support networks truly prove your worth as invaluable assets. Surrounding ourselves with positive and motivating individuals empowers us to build the strength and determination needed to overcome obstacles and persevere through tough times. When we come together, sharing our experiences and supporting one another, we can tackle life's challenges with greater ease and confidence. By working together, we can find solutions to any problem that comes our way.

Building Bridges for Success: Supportive networks not only provide emotional support and encouragement, but also open doors to new opportunities for personal growth and professional advancement. Our networks are like powerful bridges that propel us towards success, enabling us to reach our goals and fulfil our wildest aspirations! There are so many exciting ways to make this happen! You can tap into job opportunities through your professional network, seek advice from experienced mentors, or collaborate with like-minded individuals on projects and initiatives. The possibilities are endless!

In this chapter, we'll explore the many aspects of building strong networks and fostering meaningful connections in our personal and professional lives. Get ready to dive in and discover the secrets to creating powerful relationships! Get ready for an exciting session where we'll explore powerful techniques to expand our networks, foster genuine connections, and make a positive impact in our communities! Get ready to dive into a world of real-life examples, case studies, and practical activities! We'll be exploring tactics that are grounded in reality and designed to be hands-on.

8.Creating Connections

Let's dive into the exciting world of establishing connections! We want to inspire you to reflect on your support networks and brainstorm ways to enhance and expand them. This will ultimately help you better support your targets and achieve your objectives. So, let's get started! By embracing self-reflection and deepening our self-awareness, we can unlock our full potential and flourish in every area of our lives. By exploring different areas, we can uncover opportunities to forge new connections or strengthen our current relationships.

In this Chapter, I'll show you how to build strong networks and create meaningful connections that will help you thrive in our interconnected world. Get ready to take charge of your social life!

In this chapter, we're going to take things to the next level! We'll be building upon the foundation that was laid in earlier chapters, especially Chapter 7. Remember how we talked about the importance of growing your confidence and self-assurance? Well, now it's time to put those principles into action as you pursue your goals and dreams! In Chapter 8, we take what we've learned so far and build upon it with even more excitement and energy! Building strong networks is crucial for boosting and enhancing your confidence. These networks offer people a feeling of belonging, motivation, and shared experiences that boost their resilience and determination.

In this chapter, we urge you to explore the exciting potential of building strong networks and forging meaningful connections in different aspects of their lives.

In this book, you'll discover the power of surrounding yourself with people who uplift, inspire, and empower you to reach your full potential. Get ready for real-life examples, practical exercises, and deep introspection that will guide you on this transformative journey.

8.1 Illustration with example

Let's dive into the inspiring story of **Dr. Kiran Martin, a renowned social activist and the founder of Asha,** a non-profit organization dedicated to transforming the lives of those residing in Delhi's slums.

Dr. Kiran's incredible journey showcases the amazing power of building strong networks and forging meaningful connections in the pursuit of social change. It's truly inspiring to see the transformative potential that can be unlocked through these efforts. Dr. Kiran recognized the importance of building partnerships and alliances to maximize her impact as she embarked on her mission to empower marginalized communities.

With her boundless energy and unwavering determination, Dr. Kiran reached out to a wide range of individuals, organizations, and government agencies, tirelessly working to secure collaboration and support for Asha's efforts. With her extensive medical training and unwavering dedication to social justice, she was able to make a significant impact. Asha's hard work paid off as she successfully built a strong network of like-minded allies who fully supported her goals and ideals. Every single one of these allies brought their unique expertise, resources, and influence to the cause!

By fostering meaningful connections and nurturing relationships with stakeholders, Dr. Kiran effectively rallied support, raised awareness, and secured resources for Asha's programs and services. Asha has made a significant impact in enhancing healthcare, education, and community development for slum dwellers in Delhi. Through collaboration and a shared dedication to the cause, she has been able to bring about positive change.

When it comes to driving social change, Dr. Kiran's story is a powerful example of **how building supportive networks and making connections can have a transformative impact. Her ability to rally resources, involve stakeholders, and foster collaboration underscores the importance of community building and connection development in driving positive transformation.**

Call for Action: Consider the narrative of Dr. Kiran in the context of Chapter 8, you are motivated to harness the power of connection in order to bring about significant change in our own communities and beyond.

8.2 Real Life Case study

Let us take a look at the journey that **Maya, a young professional who is navigating the hurdles of growing her career in a highly competitive market, has been on.** In the quest of both personal and professional development, the narrative of Maya shows the transforming potential of networking and the cultivation of meaningful connections.

Maya is aware of the significance of establishing a solid support network in order to successfully navigate the difficulties of her business and progress her career. In a determined and foresighted manner, she actively searches out opportunities to connect with persons who share similar values and who are able to provide her with direction, support, and a different point of view.

In order to broaden her professional circle and establish new connections, Maya participates in a variety of networking activities, including conferences, business seminars, and other similar gatherings. Maya cultivates genuine relationships with peers and industry professionals by engaging in talks with them, discussing ideas with them, and sharing experiences with them. These relationships have the potential to eventually lead to important opportunities and partnerships.

Maya is aware of the significance of mentorship in her professional development, and as a result, she makes it a point to actively seek out mentorship programs and opportunities to gain knowledge from seasoned professionals working in her area. Maya receives invaluable insights, advice, and support from seasoned industry professionals through the process of mentorship. This assist her in navigating problems, establishing career goals, and making decisions that are based on accurate information.

Internet Communities: In addition to engaging in face-to-face networking, Maya makes use of online communities, forums, and social media platforms in order to establish connections with professionals located all over the world. By participating in online networking, Maya is able to broaden her sphere of influence, gain access to a variety of viewpoints, and remain current on the latest developments and trends in the industry. As a result, she is able to deepen her knowledge and increase her network of support.

Developing Meaningful Connections: Maya places a high priority on authenticity, empathy, and mutual respect in her relationships with her co-workers, mentors, and industry leaders as she works to develop meaningful connections with them. Developing trust and rapport with others, improving her relationships, and cultivating a sense of camaraderie within her professional network are all things that Maya accomplishes through the practice of actively listening, providing assistance, and bringing value to others.

Opening Doors to prospects Maya is able to broaden her network of support and open doors to new prospects for professional development and advancement in her career as a result of her proactive approach to networking and relationship-building. Through her connections, Maya is able to gain access to significant resources, ideas, and experiences that move her forward in her career journey. This is true whether she is collaborating on a project, landing a new position, or securing a chance to be mentored.

When it comes to achieving success in both one's personal and professional life, the narrative of Maya highlights the significance of establishing supportive networks and fostering meaningful connections.

Call for Action: Take proactive actions to expand your own networks, cultivate honest relationships, and create possibilities for growth and advancement in your lives.

This inspiration comes about as you reflect on Maya's path.

8.3 Discovery Exercise: Networking Goals

When you are actively attempting to extend your network and cultivate meaningful connections, one of the most important steps is to establish goals for your networking endeavours

.

Step 1: Establishing Detailed Objectives for Networking that are both specific and attainable for your networking attempts. It is important that these objectives be SMART, which stands for specific, measurable, attainable, relevant, and time-bound.
Some Examples of Objectives in Networking:

- Attend Networking Events
- Expand your involvement and exposure on professional networking platforms such as LinkedIn.
- Look for Opportunities to Be Mentored
- Join Associations for Professionals with and make it a goal to join and actively participate in groups that are significant to your interests.
- Make it a priority to enhance your relationships with your co-workers and colleagues
- Add Value: Make it a goal to add value to your network by helping, insights, or resources to other people.

Step 2: develop a structured action plan that outlines the activities you will take in order to accomplish these goals.

Step 3: Constantly examine your networking goals and track your progress towards reaching them.

Step 4: Celebrate your Accomplishments and Milestones as you make progress toward your networking goals

Networking goals are absolutely crucial in this chapter! You lay the foundation for establishing connections that will truly enhance and support your life and career. It's all about making those valuable connections!

In the earlier chapters, especially Chapter 7, we explored the importance of building confidence and self-assurance while pursuing our goals and dreams. These themes are closely connected to the topics we'll be diving into in Chapter 8. Building strong support networks is crucial for maintaining and enhancing your confidence. These networks are like a lifeline, connecting people and giving them a sense of belonging, encouragement, and shared experiences that fuel resilience and determination.

This book empowers you to create strong networks and build meaningful connections, allowing you to thrive in every area of your live

9.Celebrating Success: Recognizing Milestones and Achievements

It is crucial that we take a moment to halt and acknowledge our progress as we navigate the twists and turns that life throws at us, regardless of how insignificant or substantial it may appear to be.

In the context of this chapter, networking goals serve as a foundational component in the process of establishing connections that contribute to the enhancement and support of one's life and career.

The topics that were discussed in earlier chapters, particularly Chapter 7, where the you were encouraged to acquire confidence and self-assurance as you followed your objectives and dreams, are intricately tied to the topics that are discussed in Chapter 8. It is vital to construct supportive networks in order to maintain and improve this confidence. These networks provide individuals with a sense of belonging, encouragement, and shared experiences that strengthen their resilience and resolve.

It provides you with a road map that enables you to construct supportive networks and cultivate meaningful connections that enable you to flourish in all aspects of your life.

The ninth chapter of this book is where we begin our introspective investigation into the value of commemorating our accomplishments and acknowledging the milestones that we have reached along the way. It is crucial that we take a moment to halt and acknowledge our progress as we navigate the twists and turns that life throws at us, regardless of how insignificant or substantial it may appear to be.

Throughout the course of this chapter, we look into the significance of adopting a mindset that is characterized by appreciation and reflection, as well as the transformational potential of sharing our success stories with other people. We shed light on the enormous impact that celebrating accomplishment may have on our general well-being and sense of fulfilment by drawing from a variety of moving instances and anecdotes from real life.

Come along with us as we explore the core of Chapter 9 and learn about the transforming impact of recognizing our accomplishments and paying tribute to the significant milestones that we have reached on our journey toward personal and professional development.

9.1 Illustration with example

An illustrative and dramatic illustration of the transformational power of celebration is provided by the artistic accomplishment of **A.R. Rahman.** The following is an in-depth analysis of the ways in which Rahman's journey is connected to the topics discussed in this chapter:

The significance of commemorating important accomplishments is brought to light by Rahman's historic victory at the Academy Awards in 2009. He made history by becoming the first Indian composer to win two Oscars in the same year. The fascinating music that he composed for the film "Slumdog Millionaire" not only won him tremendous accolades and recognition for his outstanding talent and inventiveness, but it also captivated people all over the world.

Winning two Academy Awards was not only a significant achievement for Rahman in his professional life, but it was also a profoundly personal victory for him. It is a testament to the strength of determination, dedication, and artistic excellence that he rose from humble origins to achieve global fame. Through the celebration of his accomplishments, Rahman not only paid tribute to his own laborious efforts and ability, but he also motivated a great number of young musicians and artists to pursue their aspirations with the same level of passion and commitment.

India's rich musical tradition and artistic talent were brought to the attention of the world as a result of Rahman's victory at the Academy Awards, which was a momentous occasion for the Indian television industry. The pleasure and love that the Indian community feels for Rahman's success on a global scale is shown in the extraordinary celebration that was held in Chennai, the city in where Rahman was born and raised, to celebrate his accomplishment. The relevance of celebrating success is highlighted by this cultural impact, not only for the purpose of achieving personal fulfilment, but also for the wider significance of achievement in terms of encouraging others and breaking down boundaries.

The route that Rahman took to achieve Oscar glory continues to serve as a source of motivation and inspiration for aspiring musicians and artists all around the world. This exemplifies the transforming potential of making success a source of inspiration and motivation. His accomplishments not only served as a reminder of the significance of patience, ingenuity, and endurance in the pursuit of one's aspirations, but they also cleared the way for wider recognition of Indian talent on the international arena.

To sum everything up, **A.R. The creative triumph that Rahman achieved at the Academy Awards is a prime example of the significance of commemorating success and acknowledging significant milestones and accomplishments along the path of personal and professional development through celebrating success.**

Call for Action: It motivated people all around the world to dream extraordinarily and pursue their passions with unyielding tenacity. It is a monument to the transformative power of celebration that Rahman's narrative serves as an example of how it can promote motivation, resilience, and a sense of fulfilment in our lives. Reflect on it in your own life.

9.2 Real Life Case study

Aman's story is a captivating example of how celebrating can bring about incredible transformations, emphasizing the importance of acknowledging achievements and reaching milestones. Now, we're going to dive into how

9.Celebrating Success

Aman's experience relates to the topics we've covered in this chapter!

With immense dedication and meticulous planning spanning several months, Aman has triumphantly secured the job of his dreams, marking a monumental milestone in his professional journey. Aman doesn't just rush to the next objective; instead, he takes a moment to reflect on the significance of this achievement before moving forward. Aman's recognition of his achievement in landing his dream job highlights the importance of his hard work and the progress he has made on his journey towards a successful career.

By embracing his accomplishments, Aman cultivates a positive mindset and attitude towards his career. Aman can boost his sense of accomplishment and boost his confidence by taking a moment to celebrate his achievements and sharing the joy with loved ones. Aman's overall state of being is greatly enhanced by this positive perspective, which also fuels his drive to achieve greatness in his career.

Aman's celebration of his accomplishment fuels his momentum and ignites his motivation to keep pushing towards his professional goals. When Aman celebrates success, he feels an incredible rush of positive emotions and a strong sense of accomplishment. This fuels his ambition and inspires him to set new goals and reach even greater heights in his work. To ensure Aman's ongoing professional growth and accomplishment, it is crucial for him to sustain his motivation to excel.

Furthermore, **Aman's decision to celebrate his achievement with loved ones contributes to fostering a culture of celebration in both his personal and professional spheres.** Aman excels at nurturing his relationships with the people he cares about. He effortlessly expresses his happiness and gratitude towards them, creating a strong network of support. This network not only motivates him to celebrate his future accomplishments and milestones, but also adds an extra layer of joy to his journey. Aman's sense of belonging and fulfilment are enhanced by this vibrant culture of celebration, leading to a boost in his overall satisfaction and joy.

Let's dive into the importance of pausing and celebrating the journey, while also recognizing the significance of every milestone along the way!

Call for Action: Follow Aman's example and embrace the practice of celebrating achievement in their own lives.

This includes acknowledging the value of your work and discovering motivation to continue pursuing their goals with passion and drive.

9.3 Discovery Exercise: Reflection & Gratitude

The act of reflecting on one's life and expressing thanks is an essential component in the process of cultivating a sense of appreciation and contentment. Let's investigate the ways in which this practice is related to the topics discussed in the chapter:

9.Celebrating Success

Step 1: Taking a Moment to Consider Recent Achievements: Take a time to think about the recent achievements and milestones that you have achieved.

Step 2: Making a Statement of Appreciation for Support: Show thanks to the individuals and resources that have helped you along your path to achievement and encourage you to communicate your appreciation.

Step 3: Building a Sense of Appreciation Through Practice: Create a sense of appreciation for the possibilities and triumphs that have come your way in your life by acknowledging the contributions of others as well as recognizing your own efforts.

Step 4: Increasing Happiness and a Sense of Meaning in Life: Engaging in activities such as appreciation and reflection can make a big contribution to the overall sense of contentment and well-being that you experience.

Step 5: Encouragement of Ongoing Development and Achievement: Continue your pursuit of growth and achievement with tools for personal and professional development, such as gratitude and reflection.

This practice fosters a sense of fulfilment, well-being, and continuous growth and success. It encourages you to reflect on your recent accomplishments, express gratitude for support, and create a strong sense of appreciation

9.4 Discovery Exercise: sharing success stories

The act of sharing success stories plays a vital role in fostering a sense of pride and accomplishment. Let us investigate the ways in which this practice is consistent with the ideas presented in the chapter:

Step 1: Discuss your Possibilities for Achievement: share your success stories with your networks, whether it be through social media platforms, professional networking sites, or personal chats with friends and family.

Step 2: Inspiring Others Through the Sharing of Success Stories. When you openly celebrate your accomplishments, you act as role models for those who may be attempting to overcome difficulties or who may be facing challenges that are comparable to something you have experienced.

Step 3: Reiterating the Value of Personal Pride and Accomplishment. The act of publicly sharing success stories enables you to reaffirm your own sense of pride and accomplishment. A celebration like this not only helps you feel more confident in yourself, but it also inspires you to keep pushing yourself to achieve the highest possible standards in whatever you do.

Step 4: Contributing to the Cultivation of a Culture of Celebration. When people publicly acknowledge and celebrate your accomplishments, it inspires others to do the same. The culture of celebration helps to cultivate a sense of camaraderie and mutual support among the students in the same class.

9.Celebrating Success

Step 5: Facilitating Positive Engagement and Connection Within Communities : The act of sharing success stories can inspire meaningful conversations and develop connections. This can be accomplished through the exchange of congratulatory messages from peers, words of support from mentors, or experiences from other individuals who have achieved similar levels of success.

Let's reflect on our own experiences of achievement, no matter how big or small you may be. It's important to recognize the hard work and dedication that went into accomplishing your goals. You can truly embrace the incredible journey you've embarked on and the growth you've experienced by simply recognizing your accomplishments.

To develop a mindset filled with abundance, strength, and happiness, the chapter suggests that you should wholeheartedly embrace the habit of celebrating milestones and recognizing achievements. This will serve as a powerful motivation for you to continue doing so. You not only rejoice in your accomplishments, but you also cultivate a deep sense of gratitude and satisfaction, fuelling your drive for personal and professional growth. It's all about honouring your hard work and celebrating your victories!

Chapter 9 is closely linked to the preceding chapters, especially Chapter 8, which focused entirely on building meaningful connections and establishing supportive networks. When we share our successes, we love to spread the word among our networks! It's such a great way to motivate others and build a strong sense of community and support. When you recognize the power of celebrating your successes and fostering a community of support and encouragement, you can amplify your achievements and create a culture of connection.

In this chapter, I'm here to give you an exciting road map that will help you celebrate your accomplishments and acknowledge your successes in both your personal and professional life. Get ready for an incredible journey! By reflecting on personal experiences, embracing celebration, and recognizing the importance of connection, you can cultivate a mindset of appreciation, resilience, and joy. This mindset will fuel your motivation and drive you towards ongoing growth and fulfilment.

10.Beyond Limits: Sustaining Growth and Transformation/New Possibilities

There are no boundaries except the ones we create for ourselves!

As we wrap up our journey, Chapter 10 takes us on a thrilling exploration of sustaining growth and embracing fresh opportunities. Get ready for an exhilarating finale! In this chapter, we explore the exciting ways individuals can grow and thrive, drawing inspiration from real-life examples, historical figures, and the timeless wisdom of ancient India.

Throughout our journey, we've uncovered the incredible impact of coaching, self-discovery, resiliency, and joy. It's been an exhilarating experience! Now, let's take our educational experiences to the next level and push ourselves beyond our limits. There are no boundaries except the ones we create for ourselves!

As we move forward in this chapter, we'll make exciting connections between our past adventures and the path that awaits us. Every step of the journey has played a vital role in setting the foundation for the exciting adventure that awaits, from the profound process of self-discovery to the exhilarating moments of celebrating achievements. Let's dive into some real-life examples, historical figures, and timeless wisdom to shed light on the way forward!

Let's kickstart our journey by recognizing the seeds of growth and change that have been sown along the way. It all begins with reflecting on the path we've travelled so far and pinpointing those very seeds. Just like a lotus flower that rises from the depths and blossoms with breath-taking beauty, let's explore the incredible power of persistent effort and unwavering resilience in bringing about transformative change in our lives and society. Get ready for an incredible journey, just like the blooming lotus flower!

Get ready to embark on an exciting journey into uncharted territory, fuelled by the spirit of exploration and creativity! Get ready for an exciting lesson where we'll explore the incredible power of embracing new possibilities. We'll dive into the stories of fearless pioneers who defied tradition and achieved unexpected success. Get ready to be inspired!

Let's talk about connecting with others! As we go on our journey, we'll create a beautiful tapestry of connections with fellow travellers. These connections will give us strength and make our journey even more meaningful. Just like the individual strands of a tapestry, we'll explore how building meaningful connections can fuel our growth and amplify our impact.

Celebrate the Journey: Finally, it's time to stop and acknowledge the important milestones and achievements that have marked our journey. Times of celebration are a powerful reminder of the progress we've made and fuel our determination to keep pushing forward! They shine brightly, guiding us through the darkest of times.

During our exciting journey, we've delved into the incredible impact of coaching, self-discovery, conquering limiting beliefs, embracing authenticity, building resilience, empowering dreams, fostering confidence, cultivating relationships, and celebrating achievements. Right now, we're incorporating these lessons into our efforts to keep up the momentum and venture into exciting new directions.

Looking back at the incredible journey we've been on and pinpointing key areas for growth and transformation is the initial step towards sustaining our amazing progress. Let's draw inspiration from Mahatma Gandhi's lifetime dedication to self-improvement and social change as we explore the power of persistent work and unwavering dedication in bringing about profound personal and societal transformations!

10.1 Illustration with example

Mahatma Gandhi's life is a remarkable testament to continuous growth and transformation. This project aims to show the incredible power of personal dedication and determination in sparking transformative change. Gandhi's unwavering commitment to self-reflection, nonviolence, and tenacity transformed not only his own life, but also inspired millions to rally behind India's quest for freedom.

Gandhi's personal growth and development were greatly influenced by his consistent practice of self-reflection. He consistently examined his beliefs, mindset, and behaviour through introspection, aiming to align them with his principles of truth and nonviolence. Gandhi truly showcased the incredible power of self-awareness and self-improvement through his personal journey of confronting his own shortcomings and evolving as a remarkable individual.

Gandhi's strategy for social and political transformation was built upon the powerful foundation of nonviolence, also known as "ahimsa." Gandhi's remarkable ability to confront oppressive systems of colonial power and create a movement rooted in compassion and empathy was truly awe-inspiring. He advocated for peaceful resistance and civil disobedience, which became the driving force behind his transformative efforts. His unwavering commitment to nonviolence not only transformed the struggle for Indian independence, but also left an indelible mark on countless movements for justice and equality across the globe.

Gandhi remained unwavering in his pursuit of freedom and justice, even in the face of immense opposition and struggle. With an unyielding spirit, he faced countless challenges, including imprisonment, persecution, and personal sacrifices. His resilience inspired others to join the fight and fuelled the momentum of the independence movement. Gandhi's remarkable ability to persevere in the face of challenging circumstances serves as a powerful example of the incredible strength that can be attained through unwavering dedication and hard work.

The life story of Gandhi resonates deeply with the topics, as it embodies the ideals of sustaining progress and embracing new possibilities. **Gandhi's remarkable ability to rise above his own limitations and serve as a driving** force for a movement that forever changed the course of history was fuelled by his unwavering commitment to self-reflection, nonviolence, and relentless determination. Thanks to his incredible legacy, we are constantly reminded of the power of sustainable growth and transformation in creating a better world. It's not just possible, it's absolutely necessary.

> Call for Action: What are some ways in which Gandhi's values of self-reflection, non-violence, and tenacity might motivate you to maintain your own growth and transformation, as well as to welcome new opportunities in your life?

10.2 Real Life Case study

It is necessary to be open to new possibilities in order to maintain progress and bring about transformation. The tale of **Ratan Tata** is illustrative of how having the courage to travel into new area may result in the development of remarkable innovations and achievements.

The innovative vision of Ratan Tata Ratan Tata, who served as the chairman of Tata Sons in the past, exhibited a visionary approach to business that was distinguished by daring and inventiveness. In the Indian business scene, his willingness to challenge traditional knowledge and explore new pathways laid the groundwork for a transformational change that changed the landscape itself.

One of the most noteworthy undertakings that Ratan Tata engaged in was the introduction of the Tata Nano, which became well known as the "world's cheapest car." Tata, recognizing the need for inexpensive transportation in India, envisioned a vehicle that would transform mobility for millions of people. This car would be a ground-breaking innovation.

When it came to opening up new horizons, the Tata Nano was more than simply a car; it was a symbol of the democratization of transportation and the empowerment of the public. At the same time as Tata opened up new opportunities for economic mobility and social inclusion, it also made car ownership accessible to a larger portion of the people.

Although the Tata Nano was developed with the Indian market in mind, its influence was felt well beyond the limits of each individual nation. Other sectors were driven to reconsider their business models and investigate new potential for growth as a result of Tata's pioneering approach to manufacturing and distribution, which also inspired other industries to innovate.

The narrative of Ratan Tata serves as a potent reminder of the significance of being open to new opportunities and taking calculated risks in order to pursue innovation and advancement.

You are encouraged to challenge traditional thinking, venture outside of your comfort zones, and explore new vistas for the purpose of personal and professional development.

For the purpose of self-reflection, what aspects of your life do you find yourself reluctant to open yourself up to new opportunities? In order to open up new doors of opportunity for personal development and fulfilment, how can you go past your fears and uncertainties?

Call for Action: Identify one area of your life in which you feel that limiting ideas are causing you to feel stuck or confined. Develop a list of three prospective new chances or possibilities that could result in a positive change in this area. Begin by taking a baby step toward exploring each possibility, and then note how this brings forth new opportunities for personal development and transformation.

10.3 Discovery Exercise: Mind Mapping for newer possibilities

The practice of mind mapping is yet another useful activity that can help you discover new possibilities and broaden your perspective at the same time. In order to investigate fresh opportunities, you can develop a mind map in the following manner:

Step 1: Establish a central idea: Make a note of a core topic or area of interest that you want to investigate and write it down.

Step 2: Extend Your Reach: With the major notion as your starting point, draw branches that radiate outward to depict several features or components that are related to your theme. Possible opportunities, abilities that you would like to improve, resources that you require, and prospective challenges that you might face are all examples of these.

Step 3. Investigate the Connections Here: During the process of adding branches to your mind map, you should be on the lookout for connections between various thoughts and concepts.

Step 4. Come up with New Ideas: Make use of the many branches of your mind map in order to come up with new ideas and alternatives.

Step 5. Continue to Extend and Refine: As you investigate new opportunities and perspectives, the mental map you have created should be continuously expanded and refined.

Step 6. Consider and prioritize the following: After you have taken a step back, you should think about the ideas and possibilities that you have discovered

Step 7. Plan of action: Make use of your mind map as a navigational guide for acting. Create a list of specific actions that you may take in order to investigate and pursue the new opportunities that you have discovered. The creation of a mind map will not only allow you to broaden your thinking and investigate new possibilities, but it will also provide you with clarity and guidance regarding how to bring your thoughts into the actual world.

As we near the conclusion of our journey through the chapters of development, change, and opportunity, we stand on the cusp of an exciting new beginning! With the conclusion of this chapter, we have reached the peak of our investigation. It has propelled us to explore beyond the limits of our imagination and embrace the boundless opportunities that lie ahead.

Throughout our journey, every chapter has given us a treasure trove of knowledge and insight, guiding us towards self-discovery, resilience, and empowerment. It's incredible how everything comes together! Together, we've embarked on a journey of self-discovery and growth, exploring the depths of our inner selves and reaching for the stars of our dreams. Along the way, we've uncovered our hidden potential and now, it's time to revel in our achievements.

Let's dive headfirst into the realm of endless possibilities! Embracing new possibilities may come with its fair share of challenges, but it is through facing adversity that we truly discover our inner strength and resilience. With the bold decisions made by trailblazers like Ratan Tata and the imaginative pursuits of those forging their own way, we are reminded that innovation and progress lie within all of us, ready to be cultivated and grown.

Building a Strong Connection: Throughout our journey, we've formed meaningful bonds with both others and ourselves. These connections have empowered us to navigate the highs and lows we've faced along the way. Just like the intricate network of roots that fuels the growth of a mighty tree, our hopes and ambitions are built upon the strong foundation of our relationships and communities.

Let's celebrate the journey! We're so grateful for the lessons we've learned, the obstacles we've conquered, and the victories we've achieved. It's time to acknowledge the milestones and successes that have shaped our growth. Cheers to that! Every triumph showcases our unwavering perseverance, our unwavering resolve, and our unwavering belief in the boundless possibilities that reside within the human soul.

Listen up, folks! It's time to make a move! As we near the end of this leg of our adventure, we've got to carry all the wisdom and insights we've acquired into the next phase of our growth. Embrace the boundless opportunities that lie ahead on this exciting journey, and let's continue to welcome the adventure that knows no limits.

The journey is what truly shapes us, not the destination. It's about the incredible experiences we've had, the meaningful connections we've made, and the dreams we've pursued. Let's keep moving forward with courage, curiosity, and determination, knowing that every step brings us closer to unlocking our true potential and building a world full of meaning, enthusiasm, and possibilities.

Gratitude

In India, we say 'Dhanyavad' to express gratitude, a word that carries the weight of a thousand suns.

Thanks for being interested and helping! We really value you being a part of our journey. If you want to get in touch with us about anything else, here are our contact information:

Web address:

Visit our website at www.shiprasingh.com to learn more about the author.

Visit our website, www.skature.com to know the services and products we offer.

Send an email: Do you have any questions or ideas? You can email us at shipra@skature.com

Many thanks,

Shipra Singh

Self-Reflection Notes:

9 798894 155593